GOING OVER ALL THE
HURDLES
A LIFE OF
OATESS ARCHEY

GOING OVER ALL THE **HURDLES**

John Beineke

A LIFE OF

OATESS ARCHEY

INDIANA HISTORICAL SOCIETY PRESS • INDIANAPOLIS 2008

Printed in Canada

This book is a publication of the
Indiana Historical Society Press
Eugene and Marilyn Glick Indiana History Center
450 West Ohio Street
Indianapolis, Indiana 46202-3269 USA
www.indianahistory.org
Telephone orders 1-800-447-1830
Fax orders 1-317-234-0562
Online orders @ http://shop.indianahistory.org

The paper in this publication meets the minimum requirements of American National
Standard for Information Sciences—Permanence of Paper for Printed Library Materials,
ANSI Z39. 48–1984

Library of Congress Cataloging-in-Publication Data

Beineke, John A.
  Going over all the hurdles : a life of Oatess Archey / John A. Beineke.
     p. cm.
  Includes bibliographical references and index.
  ISBN 978-0-87195-260-8 (cloth : alk. paper)
  1. Archey, Oatess Eugene, 1937- 2. Marion (Ind.)–Biography.
  3. African Americans–Indiana–Marion–Biography. 4. Teachers–Indiana–Marion–Biography.
  5. Coaches (Athletic)–Indiana–Marion–Biography.
  6. United States. Federal Bureau of Investigation–Officials and employees–Biography.
  7. Sheriffs–Indiana–Grant County–Biography. I. Title.

CT275.A812B45 2008
977.2'69043092--dc22
[B]

                                                                    2007037722

A publication from the Eli Lilly Indiana History Book Fund

To my wife, Marla Krueger Beineke

Contents

Preface

This book about Oatess Archey was written for young adult readers. I hope, though, that readers of all ages will become engaged in the life of this remarkable man. The novelist Thomas B. Costain once wrote that history is made as much in the communities and lives of common people as in the palaces and castles of the privileged. While by no means a common man, Archey and his story connect to the themes of service, education, and leadership. His life began in an ordinary midwestern town and reached the highest levels of American government and society.

Archey is an African American. It has been said by many, and holds true I believe, that race has been the major issue of American history. Race will play a central role in the telling of this story. But there will be additional themes. How a man overcomes obstacles—hurdles if you will—in his life to succeed. Yet, it is more than a story of success. Many women and men in our society could be called successful. On the road to success, Archey was able to make a difference in the lives of those he touched.

The Archey story is an American story. And so it will address key historical events through the life of one man. National issues, such as integration, will be played out in an Indiana community. The economic, political, and social changes that took place in the latter half of the twentieth century will be mirrored in Archey's life.

The word hurdle will be used in this book both symbolically and athletically. As a symbol, it will embody the barriers that Archey had to overcome throughout his life. The hurdle, as an obstacle in a track-and-field event, will also represent a moment of achievement that exemplified his entire life. Archey not only went over hurdles, but he taught others how to go over them, too. That is how a life truly makes a difference.

To hurdle means to go over something, but it also can mean to go forward or make progress. All people are confronted with barriers in their lives. Some choose to go around those barriers, while others have no choice but to go over them. Archey made the choice in his life to go over the hurdles—all the hurdles.

* * *

Observing a Life

Within these pages the voice of a witness, observer, and sometime participant in the story of Oatess Archey will emerge. The purpose is not to focus attention on that individual, who also happens to be the author of this book. Rather it is to provide a close-up perspective. It is what one individual saw—sometimes close and sometimes from afar. How an adolescent, young man, and man viewed another person will add a dimension that otherwise would not be present.

Born a dozen years after Archey into a white, working, middle-class family, my observations of this man are done under a different lens than others. Yet it will also be representative of the other young people I grew up with and who are now in middle age. I hope that these brief observations, spaced throughout the book, will give the reader an idea of how one person, maybe even the age of the reader, viewed this man and the effect he had on his life.

1

🏃

The Importance of Roots

Much of Oatess Archey's life story—athlete, teacher, coach, Federal Bureau of Investigation (FBI) agent, sheriff, and leader—occurs in the city of Marion, Indiana. Located sixty-five miles northeast of the state capital of Indianapolis, Marion is a modest-sized city. The community is situated on a mainly level plain, with the occasional slight hill, through which runs the Mississinewa River. In 1825 a settler named Martin Boots founded the town. He received the land through a charter that was signed by the sixth president of the United States, John Quincy Adams.

Within ten years there appeared in Marion a courthouse, a school, several churches, and even a jail. Both a school and a city street would later be named for the pioneering Boots. The name Marion had its roots from the American Revolutionary hero, Francis Marion. Also known as the Swamp Fox, Marion utilized hit-and-run guerilla tactics against the British army in the colony of South Carolina.

Agriculturally based, as were most such towns in the 1800s, Marion eventually grew into a commercial center for Grant County. There was the indispensable mill to process grain, various stores, banks, and other economic interests. African Americans moved to Grant County in the 1840s, eventually founding a village named Weaver.

The descendants of those families from the early Weaver days can still be found in a modern Marion telephone directory. The names include Pettiford, Gulliford, Stewart, Burden, and Ward. Eventually most blacks living in Weaver migrated to Marion as they followed the course of economic opportunity from the farm to the factories and other professions.

A number of notable persons either passed through or had connections to Marion. The composer and musician, Cole Porter, traveled from nearby Peru to take music lessons at the local conservatory. Willis Van Devanter, a U.S. Supreme Court justice from 1911 to 1937, attended the local schools. After law school in Cincinnati, he practiced in Marion for three years before moving to Wyoming. John and Robert Kennedy both visited Marion in their runs for the presidency. Samuel Plato, an African American architect, designed a number of public and private buildings from 1910 to 1940 that were of national note. James Dean, Hollywood actor of the 1950s, was born in Marion and attended school in the nearby town of Fairmount.

It would be paths and roads emerging from various directions that eventually led Oatess Archey's maternal great-grandparents, grandparents, and parents to Marion. Oatess's great-grandfather, John Boyd, had migrated to Indiana from Jackson, Tennessee, through Hopkinsville, Kentucky, by foot, bicycle, and train. The Boyd family had made this move searching for a better life—a place less oppressive than the South at this time. It was the 1890s and John Boyd lived at 1709 South Meridian Street in Marion. He earned his living mainly as a cobbler, repairing shoes and running an ice cream parlor.

Although Boyd had come to the North in order to experience more freedom, a tragic act of violence ended his dream of a better life. He had worked several years in Marion, successfully establishing his shoe repair and ice cream businesses. It was not uncommon, however, for whites to intimidate blacks in a variety of ways—socially, politically, and economically. And on occasion the intimidation became physical.

On the evening of August 23, 1897, Boyd was fatally shot and killed by a Marion city police patrolman, Tony George (George later became Marion's police chief and Grant County sheriff). When Patrolman George went on his evening rounds, he was told there had been some type of disturbance at the Boyd residence that afternoon. According to Albert Milton, who witnessed what followed, an altercation erupted between the officer and the Boyd family. Heated words were exchanged, with the Boyds insisting that there had been no trouble at the house that day. When the dispute turned physical, the patrolman pulled his gun and fatally shot Boyd.

Witnessing the entire traumatic incident was Boyd's twenty-two-year-old son, Thomas, whom the family called Tob. Reflecting on the event, related to him by family members through the years, Oatess Archey said, "This was quite a tragic event in Tob Boyd's life." Others would not be as even-handed or understated in their assessment of the episode as the great-grandson. Some bluntly maintained that a black man's life was not "worth a hill of beans" in Marion—or in most towns in the United States at the beginning of the twentieth century.

Marion mayor Von Behren decided that the shooting had been in self-defense and no charges were made against George. Whether for legal or humanitarian reasons, the city of Marion did compensate Boyd's family. The city decided to give young Tob Boyd a lifetime job with the Marion Street Department. This act may have been taken to salve the consciences of the city officials. Or perhaps the gesture was made to provide a job and means of making a living for the victim's son. Such compensation by the local authorities, though, could not begin to offset the loss of a man's life.

Tob Boyd began what would be his lifetime work of pushing a broom, cleaning the streets around the city square. Later, the street department secured a mechanical street sweeper. But Boyd was still given the menial job of sitting on the front of the street sweeper, pushing debris into the machine. His white counterparts drove the sweeper. He worked at his post for sixty years. City administration after administration continued Boyd's employment, probably forgetting why this aging man was even on the payroll.

In 1960 a new mayor asked, "Who is this old codger?" Boyd, then eighty-five years old, said he had been told that he had lifetime employment with the street department. His protest, however, fell on deaf ears, and Boyd was let go from the only job he had ever known. Three months later, in July of 1960, he was dead.

During his days in Marion, Boyd had remembered that in Tennessee when he was a boy one could always tell where black families lived. Whites often had two-story houses, while African Americans lived in one-story shacks. On his modest salary and building it himself, Boyd lived in a beautiful two-story home, in a way casting off this stigma from his past. A life of hard work had left this legacy to his family.

Oatess Archey's father's family arrived in Indiana from Virginia by way of North Carolina. This was a common route to the Hoosier state for both blacks and whites from the eighteenth century on. Originally the Archey family name had been Archer. At some point in its journey, the family came into contact with a group of Quakers, a religious denomination known for pacifism, tolerance, and disciplined life. Quakers were one of the first religious groups to champion abolitionism, sharing with blacks a history of persecution and exile. For some unknown reason, the Quakers in Indiana dropped the *r* for a *y*, changing Archer to Archey.

It was the early 1930s and the United States was in the grip of the Great Depression. With the unemployment rate at 25 percent, having work was never taken for granted. But Oakley Archey was one of the fortunate men who had a job. Working as part of a traveling road construction crew from Henry County, Oakley happened to be working in the neighborhood where Tob Boyd lived. He had stopped at 1709 South Meridian Street and went to the front door in search of a drink of cold water. Orpha, Boyd's daughter, opened the front door and gave Oakley a glass of water. As Oatess later told the story, it was "love at first sight." Oakley gave up the itinerant work of building roads, settled in Marion, and married Orpha.

Oatess Eugene Archey was born in Marion in 1937. His older brother, Thomas, or Tom as he was known, had been born two years earlier. The world in the summer of 1937 was an unsettled place both on the domestic front and on the international scene. The Spanish Civil War, what some have called the dress rehearsal for World War II, had begun the year before. Fascists, communists, socialists, and democrats fought for control of the Iberian Peninsula. Japan had invaded China and even attacked the U.S. gunboat, *Panay*. German dictator, Adolf Hitler, had reoccupied the Rhineland in 1936, annexed Austria in 1938, and invaded Czechoslovakia and Poland in 1939. World War II had begun.

In 1937 Franklin Delano Roosevelt had been inaugurated for his second term as president of the United States. He faced an ongoing economic depression that had been lessened somewhat by a number of government programs he had put in place known as the New Deal. But there was still turmoil amongst the population that year. Autoworkers staged a successful sit-down strike at the General Motors plant in Flint, Michigan. In addition, agriculture in the South was being radically changed by the introduction of a mechanical cotton picker. Once silent or hidden minorities began to question the system—segregation—they had toiled under for generations. At the urging of First Lady Eleanor Roosevelt, black education and civil rights leader Mary McLeod Bethune protested openly against discriminatory hiring practices in the District of Columbia.

These events swirled around Oakley and Orpha Archey. The events affected their lives even in the seemingly sheltered small city in the heart of the Midwest. With two young sons, the couple labored hard to eke out a living in these troubled economic times. But with all of this turmoil and disruption going on about them, the Archeys were a close-knit family, held together by unwavering core values and a steady faith.

Oatess's parents were religious people attending the Allen Temple African Methodist Episcopal Church located on a triangle of land where Thirty-fifth Street met Nebraska Street in south Marion. Oatess and his brother wore bib overalls during the week. On Saturday night Orpha washed them and during the colder months dried them by the Kenmore coal stove in the family room. Sunday dress included sweaters while the rest of the week T-shirts were worn. But how the Archey family lived their lives went much deeper than what was worn on Sunday. Their values were genuinely imbedded in religious belief and practice.

The Archey family's religious roots cannot be overemphasized when seeking an explanation for their two remarkable sons and their subsequent successful careers. When trouble beckoned, Oakley responded with the saying, "The darkest hour is just before dawn." He also told his sons that "the most powerful position in the world is on your knees praying." Later in his life Oatess said that he spent much time in prayer and through it all "God took care of me."

Oatess's and Thomas's mother, Orpha, was considered a strict woman of high principles. She completed the eleventh grade, one year short of high school graduation. But for a black woman to complete high school was considered a near impossibility in that day, making her accomplishment that much more remarkable. Black women might clean houses, but obtaining any employment beyond menial labor was virtually impossible. She was the disciplinarian of the family, although the more serious infractions by her sons were dealt with by their father. Thomas and Oatess placing sand in the radiator of the family truck qualified for this special attention. Such episodes by the two Archey brothers, however, were rare.

Orpha played the piano and had a singing voice that Oatess would later liken to Mahalia Jackson's. Singing alto/contralto, she was a member of the Peerless Quartet, a women's vocal ensemble that appeared throughout Indiana, even performing on the radio. Orpha's most notable attribute, though, may have been her speaking voice. She was precise in her vocabulary and flawless in her enunciation, diction, and intonation.

* * *

I had met Oatess Archey's parents at my father's gas station in Marion. They usually stopped on Sunday afternoons. I often worked after going to church and eating lunch. Oakley would get out of his Chevrolet and order his gasoline in gallons, not by the dollar as most customers did. In the days before self-serve stations, the fuel was pumped for the customers, not by the customers.

Oakley was friendly, but reserved. I would pull down the license plate on a hinge below the trunk of the car, unscrew the gas cap, place the nozzle in the channel that led to the tank, and set it on automatic. I would then grab a sponge and chamois and begin washing the windshields and windows all the way around the car.

Orpha was always with her husband, sitting in the front seat of the car. She would nod to me when I reached her side of the car and say in a refined voice, *"Good afternoon. How are you?"* It is not surprising that a person *of color is capable of perfect enunciation, carefully selected vocabulary, or meticulous diction—it was surprising that anyone in our town spoke with such precision. And very few customers on the passenger-side of the car spoke to the gas jockey. But Orpha did. "Fine," I would say, "and how are you?" As rapidly as she greeted me she would reply, "Very good, thank you."*

My father always spoke highly of the senior Archey, who worked at the nearby Anaconda Wire and Cable factory. People in Marion in the 1960s knew and kept a "color line," but for some reason the Archeys seemed to cross it in a number of areas. As a twelve-year-old kid, though, I had no idea what crossing that line meant. But I would learn.

* * *

When he was a child, Oakley had been sitting in a highchair when his older sister tipped it over. He suffered back and neck injuries that almost killed him. Oakley's mother, Ella Archey, heard the doctor say, "That boy won't live to his twelfth year." As a result of the accident, Oakley would unpredictably hemorrhage through his nose at school. In part, due to this medical condition, his education ended at the fifth grade. Growing up, the physician's prediction reverberated in Oakley's mind and he vowed to himself, "I *will* live." And he did. In Oatess's view, his father's limited education did not imply a lack of intelligence. In fact, he viewed his father as remarkably bright. Able to read and do math, his father, according to Oatess, had a great mind that was never cultivated. Oakley entered the world of adult work by hauling coal and then was a day laborer for Bowman Construction. He eventually moved to the Anaconda Wire and Cable Company as a millwright—a master mechanic on large machines—spending twenty-six years of his working life with the company.

Orpha and Oakley Archey, circa 1979.

One day Oakley was hauling coal with a white friend whose first name by happenstance was Archie. The white man was evicting a family in north Marion at 832 East Sherman Street. The year was 1942. The United States had recently entered World War II and many blacks from the South had begun to migrate to the North for jobs in factories churning out supplies and equipment for the war effort. North Marion was an all-white enclave with only one black family, the Alexanders. Able to take advantage of this unanticipated situation, Oakley purchased the house for a bargain price of $850. But he did not really stop to think about the racial issues that might arise from living there.

The racial implications of the purchase soon became very clear to the Archey family. The family was a virtual black island in a sea of whites in this section of Marion. As a result, it seemed to Oakley and Orpha that their young sons were on display in the neighborhood. They decided to limit the boys to their own yard. This was to protect them from getting emotionally hurt by being subjected to possible verbal insults. To keep his sons occupied, Oakley set up a horseshoe pit and built a basketball court in the backyard. Kids being kids—black or white—boys from the neighborhood eventually congregated around the Archey home and were soon invited into the homemade playground. Sports became the dynamic force that broke down the race barrier.

As the Archey brothers grew older, they were hired by George Brinker, a nearby well-to-do farmer. Tom and Oatess picked corn and shocked wheat, baled hay, and cleaned out stables. The pay was seventy-five cents a day. One summer during the mid-1950s, Oatess worked at Pulleys Poultry House, killing and plucking chickens. On a normal day Oatess and two other men prepared approximately six hundred chickens. The brothers also painted and trimmed houses. Later, as teenagers, they worked during the summer months at the Anaconda factory. The work ethic, deeply embedded in the two Archey boys from birth, remained with them throughout their lives. And in spite of initial caution on the part of both blacks and whites in north Marion, the Archey family became an integral part of the community.

2

The Tree on the Courthouse Square

Racial violence was no stranger to Oatess Archey's family. The killing of his great-grandfather by a policeman was a precursor to further racial tragedy three decades later. Often the horrendous and brutal stories of violence against blacks in this country are associated with the South. Much of the cruel behavior toward freedmen after the Civil War did occur south of the Mason-Dixon Line. But there was a notable and infamous episode that took place in the North. Considered the most southern of the northern states in political, social, and racial outlook, Indiana was the location of a vicious double lynching. The place was Marion, Indiana, and the year 1930.

Both state and national antilynching movements had been advocated since the time of Reconstruction. During the period of Reconstruction (1865–77) the rope and robe of the Ku Klux Klan were used to intimidate and control black populations across the country. Whites believed that blacks needed to "know their place." The first president of the United States to speak out against such intimidation was Theodore Roosevelt, a Republican from New York. But at the beginning of the twentieth century his comments were limited and too infrequent to make any lasting impact on the general thinking about race in America.

After Roosevelt, William Howard Taft served a single term as president and was followed in the White House by Woodrow Wilson, a Democrat born in Virginia. For all his progressive tendencies, Wilson was an outright racist. He told "darkie" jokes in the White House and refused to appoint blacks to federal jobs. Wilson even provided the introductory narrative to the blatantly racist 1915 W. D. Griffith film *The Birth of a Nation* that glorified the Ku Klux Klan.

Warren G. Harding, Republican president from 1921 to 1923, did make a courageous speech on race relations in Alabama during his abbreviated term. But his successors until 1961—with the exception of Missouri Democrat Harry Truman—had little interest in questions of race or the plight of black citizens. And the same could be said for the governors in most states, both North and South. Not until 1964, under Democrat Lyndon B. Johnson's leadership, did any meaningful civil rights legislation become law. For most citizens, though, it would be local events that had the greatest effect on their lives.

On an August night in 1930 on the outskirts of Marion, a young white couple was parked in an automobile off of the main road in an area near the Mississinewa River and well known as a lover's lane. What actually occurred next will probably never be known with any certainty. Three young black men allegedly accosted the young man and woman. Of the five people on the scene that summer night only two survived. One of the black men fled the scene. The young woman in the car claimed she was raped, but some people at the time thought she was probably coached in her trial testimony. At a later trial in Anderson, Indiana, she recanted her testimony that she had been raped. Her male companion was shot and killed and the other two young black men were lynched. The accusations surrounding the case included not only rape, but also robbery and assault. The three young black men were apprehended and placed in the turreted, red-brick Grant County Jail under the supposed protection of Sheriff Jake Campbell.

A mob of undetermined size, but certainly in the thousands, became inflamed with racial hatred. While the lynching was not inspired by the Ku Klux Klan, there were active members in the crowd. The sheriff, if not an active participant, was probably a Klan sympathizer. Quickly gathering in downtown Marion, the mob was stoked on by the accusation of sexual assault on the white woman. The core group that led the lynching included twenty to thirty men. The mob soon forced its way into the jail. Little, if any, resistance was put forth by Campbell or his deputies.

The throng took Tom Shipp, age nineteen, and Abe Smith, age eighteen, across Third Street to Adams Street, one half block west of the jail, to the northeast corner of the city square. The gray-stoned Grant County Courthouse sat on this block in the center of town. Shipp was lynched first followed quickly by Smith. Both young men may have been beaten to death in the jail and their bodies displayed on the courthouse square. The third young black man, sixteen-year-old James Cameron, was also dragged to the scene by the mob. Frenzied and swarming, the horde seemed bent on murdering their third victim of the night. Years later, Cameron said that a voice, maybe even otherworldly in its source, audibly said, "Leave that boy alone." Indeed, miraculously, someone from the crowd yelled that there had been enough violence for one night. Cameron was taken back to the jail and then spirited out of town.

One witness to the events of the summer night was a young black man who, with a friend, was looking on from the top floor of the six-story Spencer House, a hotel located at the southeast corner of the square. This black adolescent watched in horror as the mob killed Shipp and Smith. The young man later become a respected professional in the community and a civic leader. But that night, as he witnessed his racial brothers having their necks broken with ropes at the hands of white men, he hid and kept quiet. It was his only choice. If they could do that to those young men, then they could do the same to him.

Historian James Madison tells of the infamous photograph taken by Lawrence Beitler, a local Marion photographer. It later appeared on postcards. The photograph of Shipp and Smith is one of the most widely reproduced depictions of lynching in American history. (Historian and commentator Alistair Cooke included it in his prize-wining history of the United States.) It is also one of the most

A crowd outside the Grant County Jail that held the three young black men accused of killing a white man and raping a white woman in Marion.

misidentified. Madison tells of it being labeled as occurring in Missouri. Since Madison's book was published, it continues to be misidentified. A recent book on the civil rights movement indicates the photograph was taken in Florida.

State officials, beginning at the top in the governor's office, reacted unconcernedly to the news of the lynching. Newspapers reported the violence, but condemnation on editorial pages was muted. Black newspapers in the state and across the nation voiced their outrage and called for investigations. A trial was held, but there were no convictions.

This episode occurred just four years after a bonfire on the opposite side of the courthouse square had celebrated a state championship for

The infamous Lawrence Beitler photograph showing the aftermath of the lynching of Tom Shipp and Abe Smith.

the city's high school basketball team. That event had also brought thousands from the community together, but in a different manner. Now, on this August night in 1930, the bodies of two young men hung from a tree. This would be a silent but effective reminder, heavy with meaning—blacks in Marion needed to remember their place. Whenever he thought about he event, "chills would run up and down" his back, Oatess remembered.

* * *

My mother was seven years old in August of 1930. But she was not in Marion the night of the lynching. She and her parents were in Wyoming visiting her father's twin brother. Would my grandfather have been present if he had been in town? Would he have taken part? The local Ku Klux Klan met on the upper floors of downtown business buildings. There may have been membership rolls, but they have never been located.

While none of my relatives were present on that night, two men who worked for my father at his gas station had been there. During the slow business times at the gas station, they each related to me what that night was like. One of them had even met his future wife that evening.

Although not taking direct part in the lawlessness, the two men had been observers to that tragic evening. One of the men told a different version of Cameron's story about his escape from the mob that night. Fire hoses were cut by the crowd to stop the law enforcement officials from attempting to break up the mob. After the first two young men had been lynched, Cameron was dragged down the street toward the square. "You have the wrong man," screamed Cameron, "I am in jail for riding trains, not for killing anybody." For some reason, that seemed to convince the leaders of the pack and they returned Cameron to the sheriff's custody.

As the two men who worked for my father told their stories—in between our pumping gas, checking oil, and cleaning windshields—there was never an opinion or judgment about the act that had taken place. Was it considered routine, even customary, to hang people in the public square? Did anyone question what was happening at that time, or in the almost four decades since the deed was done? These two men were, after all, just barely men at the time—overgrown boys really. One was from the country and the other from the city. Just innocent observers to this event one could say. Later, as a high school and college student though, I would learn to ask, as those who were present during the Holocaust asked, "Is there any difference between an observer and a participant?"

3

Growing Up Black and White

When Oatess Archey's brother Thomas began attending Washington School in north Marion—a building that housed kindergarten through ninth grade—he was often teased by the other students. One courageous teacher, Frances Brunka, called Tom aside one day and said, "Don't cry. You are a diamond in the rough—you are special. Don't let these kids get to you." Tom never forgot what this wise and compassionate woman said to him. Overcome these meaningless hassles and harassments of the classroom and playground, she advised, not by responding in kind to thoughtless bullies, but through hard work and appropriate conduct.

Oatess, two years younger than Tom, had no doubt heard of his brother's difficulties at school. He had no wish to experience them for himself. On his first day of kindergarten, Oatess attempted to make a hasty exit and retreat home after his mother had dropped him off. Ready for such a stunt, Oatess's mother intercepted him just as he made it out the schoolhouse door and down the steps. She quickly returned him to the classroom. Education was important to Orpha Archey and Oatess would be in his seat from that moment on.

In addition to what the Archey brothers had to withstand from insensitive fellow students and the occasional bully, there were

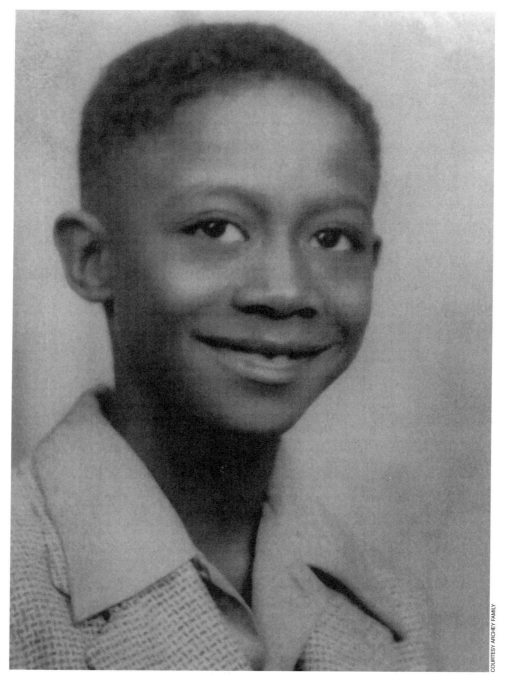

Oatess Archey, age eleven.

hardships that proved unique to them. For example, during Halloween the fun of trick or treat was to try to fool adults and other children as to one's identity. But how does a black child cover the color of the skin on his hands in a costume or his face from the sides of a mask? While seemingly insignificant to many, to Tom and Oatess it was a torturous experience at the time. Eventually, the snide and hurtful racial comments decreased as the white neighbors in north Marion became highly protective of the Archey family. There was an unspoken understanding to shield the boys from harsh verbal slights and overt acts of unkindness. And if there were hurtful remarks made toward their sons, the Archeys never related them to the two boys.

While sports eventually became an area in which racial barriers could be broken down, another was the church. Tom and Oatess attended Sunday School at the Grant Street Pilgrim Holiness Church in their neighborhood. The Pilgrim Holiness denomination eventually merged with the Wesleyan Methodist Church that had its roots in the antislavery movement of the 1840s. After leaving the all-white church, the Archey boys would ready themselves to attend their own Allen Temple African Methodist Episcopal Church, squeezing themselves into the cab of their father's one-ton truck.

Throughout their lives, the Archey brothers were unique. An example of this is as simple as how Oatess tied his shoes. As with many mothers, Orpha decided that she had tied her youngest son's shoes once too often. She told him one day that he would have to tie them himself. And so he did. After a number of failures, Oatess tied his shoes in a most distinctive and uncommon manner. But it did the job and he had done it himself. Years later when he was coaching, his eighth grade basketball team would by chance see him tie his shoelaces. They would ask him to tie them again and again as they attempted to understand exactly how he managed this simple task in such an unusual way.

Blacks, as well as whites, often asked why the Archeys lived in an all-white section of the city. The explanation was simple—Oakley had been able to secure a very good house for a remarkably low price. It did not stop black kids at Allen Temple AME Church, however, from asking Oatess and his brother, "Are you trying to be better than us by living out north?" This amazed the boys because financially they were clearly no better off than their friends in south Marion. Even Oatess's future wife, Barbara, confirmed years later that the perception of the social superiority of the Archey family was one held by many Marion blacks.

And yet, living in a white neighborhood gave Oatess rare insight into race. As an adult he reflected on his boyhood experiences, noting that there were "good whites" who protected his family and stood up for the Archey brothers when necessary. One white couple, Bill and Phyllis Hall, were almost like parents to Oatess. The usual, even uniform, ill-treatment blacks could expect from whites did not always hold for Oatess, nicknamed Odie by his friends. And this would give him a different slant on the race issue—certainly different than the opinions held by some blacks. And it changed how he viewed his work, his coaching, and his interactions as a minority within the dominant white society.

Oakley and Orpha had told their sons that they were going to have to be "better" than other children—white children—in order to succeed. This would be a common theme in many African American families. Condoleezza Rice, secretary of state for President George W. Bush, was told as a child in Alabama that she would have to work twice as hard and do twice as well as white kids to make it in American society. But at the same time, she was never to think of herself as a victim. This was the exact sentiment presented by the Archeys to their sons. Although it was plainly acknowledged as unfair, Tom and Oatess had to perform at a higher level to succeed in the classroom, acquire a job, or make it in sports.

Tom appears to have been the optimist of the two brothers, while Oatess was more the pessimist—at least when he was younger. For Tom the "way out" was always education. "Go to college, Odie," Tom encouraged his brother. And under his breath, with a tinge of skepticism, Oatess muttered, "Sure, right." But the older brother's words made their mark and Oatess has always acknowledged Tom's positive influence and encouragement.

Tom's confidence came from a teacher at Washington School, Clay Layman. A woodshop and physical education teacher, Layman also served as a coach. He gave both Archey boys the opportunity to make it in sports. Tom's chance occurred first and came in the long-distance running sport of cross country. Tall, slender, and African American, Tom was nicknamed by a teacher "the flying pretzel." Whether or not that was a racial slur is unclear. At other times there was no doubt that remarks were racial in nature. One day in Oatess's high school biology class the topic was plants, specifically fruit. The teacher told the students that he had recently read about a new variety of seedless watermelon that had been developed. "You, Oatess can really go now," cracked the teacher. The class roared with laughter. One of the most degrading stereotypes—the watermelon-eating black man—had been reinforced and given credence by a teacher. The insensitive teacher in the early 1950s was oblivious to the embarrassment he had caused his student.

The 1930 Marion lynching remained a part of the collective memory of the Marion community. The episode was mentioned in the Archey home, where the parents warned the boys to watch who they talked to and what they said. While the possibility of lynching may have been remote during the time that Tom and Oatess were growing up, the perception that such an event could occur was genuine. And it played itself out in a number of ways in everyday life.

The boys had been warned of the social taboo of interracial socializing of any kind, especially between males and females. Even the most innocent playground games were fraught with danger in their minds. Holding hands with a white girl during a playground or physical education activity was a potential crisis for Oatess. "Let's hold hands in a circle," a little white girl would say to him. Such an invitation caused Oatess's forehead to bead with sweat and start his lip twitching. "Will this get me lynched?" he thought. The Archey boys were extremely cautious in their interactions with the opposite sex at the all-white Washington School. They were terrified that they, too, would end up hanging from a tree on the courthouse square for an alleged indiscretion. On Sundays, the boys attempted to interact with the black girls at church. "While at Washington School, though, it was all books and sports with no social life," recalled Oatess.

* * *

One learns about race. It is not a concept that comes genetically encoded in our DNA. I learned about race from my family, my classmates, and the people in my neighborhood. I must say it was not until I was in high school that I seriously gave the race issue the thought I should have. An enlightened social studies teacher in my freshman year spoke openly about a number of issues that had eluded, escaped, or were purposely concealed from me as a student. One of those issues was race. All the photos on the walls in my elementary school were of white presidents—George Washington, Abraham Lincoln, and Thomas Jefferson. We studied people of color in other lands—South America was always a popular region to study. But never the history of race in our own country. Ironic when we were living through the most turbulent times in American history, the 1960s.

But if the schools dismissed the issue of race, hearing about it in my father's gas station was hard to miss. A number of customers came from Johnstown, the name for the black section of east Marion located literally "across the tracks." There seemed little attempt to even hide one's thinking on race. I heard a man say one day, "Pigs and cows don't mix, so why should coloreds and whites?" He was referring to interracial dating and marriage. One white woman told me while I was pumping gas in her Cadillac that the reason the front yards of colored families had no lawns was that "the children had unusual oil on their feet" that killed the grass. Even on a trip to a ball game with a group from my church, one man used the word "n____r," explaining that there was a difference between good coloreds and bad coloreds. "N_____s were the bad coloreds" in this man's mind. I never heard the term in my home, but I did hear it.

* * *

If the schools were not formally segregated, almost all of the other social and recreational institutions were. The Indiana and the Paramount movie theaters in downtown Marion were both segregated, requiring blacks to sit in the balcony. Two other theaters, the Luna Lite and the Lyric, were not. Oatess was able to skirt the issue of sitting separate from his white friends when attending movies by convincing his buddies it was cool to sit upstairs. The Idyl Wyld roller-skating rink and the Matter Park Swimming Pool were both segregated.

But the formal and informal patterns of segregation in the nation and in communities such as Marion would soon be broached. Race, as the major issue throughout American history, would prove a thorny and complex problem to solve. And yet a series of school desegregation cases were working their way through the federal courts just as Tom and Oatess Archey left Washington School to attend Marion High School. Each passing year race was becoming more and more difficult for Americans to ignore.

4

1954

The year 1954 proved to be a historic time, even before a landmark school desegregation decision from the U.S. Supreme Court. The French gave up trying to control one of their colonies in Southeast Asia—a small country called Vietnam. The initial study that cigarettes might be harmful to one's health was made public that year. Roger Bannister became the first man to run the mile in less than four minutes. Elvis Presley, an unknown white singer from Tupelo, Mississippi, who sounded black to many radio listeners, recorded "That's All Right (Mama)" in a Memphis studio. And a young theology school graduate, Martin Luther King Jr., became the pastor at the Dexter Avenue Baptist Church in Montgomery, Alabama.

Then in May of that year the nine black-robed Supreme Court justices handed down their *Brown v. Board of Education of Topeka* decision. Comprised of four companion suits that had been heard as early as 1950, the *Brown* case challenged the infamous sixty-year-old "separate-but-equal" ruling. In Louisiana in 1896, a light-skinned black man named Homer Plessy rode a train sitting in the "whites only" section. The train conductor, a man named Ferguson, challenged Plessy's right to the seat. The state segregation law that called for separation of the races was tested in court. The nineteenth-century

Supreme Court decree, known as *Plessy v. Ferguson*, decided that segregation was legal as long as the modes of transportation for the two races were "equal."

For the next fifty years, the *Plessy* case served as the precedent for the practice known as "separate but equal." This meant that the races could be kept separate if conditions for that division were equal. It was mainly applied in the South and not only to trains. It included many public facilities, accommodations, and institutions such as restaurants, hotels, swimming pools, universities, and public schools. By 1950 the *Plessy* case had been somewhat eroded. But it still held sway in practice, if not in law, throughout much of the land.

As Oatess Archey entered his senior year at Marion High School in 1954, there were two kinds of segregation being practiced. De facto segregation meant that blacks and whites were separated by the fact they lived in different neighborhoods or chose not to attend the same churches. De jure segregation, though, meant that blacks and whites were divided and kept apart in schools and other public facilities by law. Of the forty-eight states in the nation in 1954, seventeen mandated segregated schools, sixteen prohibited the practice, eleven had no specific laws, and four gave local school districts the option to separate the races in their schools. Indiana allowed segregated schools, but did not require it.

Linda Brown, an elementary school student living in Topeka, Kansas, had to cross a dangerous railroad track to attend a segregated school. A white school was located much closer to her home. Her father brought suit against the school board challenging the segregation law, as did parents in the states of Virginia and South Carolina. The case was argued by a National Association for the Advancement of Colored People team of lawyers. The thrust of their argument was that segregation fostered a sense of inferiority, which in turn affected the child's motivation to learn. And so the central question in the *Brown* case became: does the segregation of the races damage the learning opportunities of black students? The highest court in the land said that it did.

The *Brown* case, when it was decided in May of 1954, proved to be significant for a number of reasons. Previous cases had chiseled away at the "separate but equal" doctrine in areas such as housing, public facilities, and even higher education. But they were often local or state cases that were narrowly judged and had neither a national impact nor implementation. Obvious examples were in Texas and Oklahoma, where a separate law school and school of education, respectively, were created for a single black student each. The courts struck down these practices. But the public schools were a different matter. Since they operated in every state and community, any court ruling would have an all-encompassing, and to many whites, invasive effect on everyday life.

The lead attorney for those citizens challenging the "separate but equal" doctrine was Thurgood Marshall. Head of the Legal Defense Fund of the NAACP, Marshall went on to become a federal judge, solicitor general, and in 1965 President Lyndon B. Johnson's appointee as the first black Supreme Court justice. Marshall used a variety of arguments to challenge segregation. These included the use of black-and-white dolls demonstrating how discrimination psychologically damaged children—even in their play. Adding further meaning to the *Brown*

Thurgood Marshall.

case, the decision was unanimous. All nine white, male justices had ruled in favor of overturning the sixty-year-old convention of keeping the races apart by law as it applied to public schools.

During the first half of the twentieth century, Marion, Indiana, had a mix of segregated and nonsegregated schools. Brownlee School on Adams Street, near the downtown area, operated as a black school until the 1930s, when it was integrated with a white school. The D. A. Payne Elementary School, however, taught black children until 1954. Miss Nevada Pate was a longtime teacher with the Marion school district and the first black teacher hired for the all-black school. There did not seem to be a connection between the year and the Supreme Court case when the school on the south side of town closed its doors. The rules governing which school black students attended, though, did not seem to be rigid. Pupils apparently enrolled according to custom or the neighborhood where they lived rather than by school district policy or mandate.

This was true for the Archey brothers who lived on the all white, northeast side of Marion. Along with one other student, Oatess and Tom were the only three blacks to attend Washington School. As the Supreme Court concluded, desegregated schools had a profound impact on how students lived and learned. And this held true for the two Archey brothers in how they looked at race, life, and education.

There was, though, one major flaw in the *Brown* decision. The weakness emerged the following year in what became known as the *Brown II* decision when the court failed to establish a measurable timetable for the schools to integrate. The justices used the phase "with all deliberate speed" as the directive by which the schools would be desegregated. In the North as well as the South, the speed sought by the justices to desegregate proved exceedingly slow. The long wait lasted well into the 1970s for some school districts in the country. And the twentieth century would turn into the twenty-first century before some schools held integrated proms and other social functions.

* * *

My mother graduated from Marion High School in 1940 and I graduated from the school in 1968. Almost exactly between my mother's graduation and my own was that of Oatess Archey, who graduated in 1955. His senior year encompassed the years of the Brown v. the Board of Education *case and the subsequent* Brown II *decision. Yearbooks chronicle the events in one's high school years. They literally take a snapshot of the people, places, and highlights, capturing for all time what occurred in the lives of students and faculty. When I visit my mother I often look at her yearbooks. Who were the athletes, who were the faculty, what were the major events of the year, what might it have been like to have been a student at that time and in that place?*

I have done the same thing with the yearbook from 1955. What can one learn from such a record after half of a century? From the beginning of the yearbook one observes separation. There is a wide-angle photograph taken just before the doors of Marion High School opened to begin the day. It shows four distinct groups of high school students on the steps—white females, white males, black females, and black males. Once they moved inside the building the divisions became even more evident.

The dozens of assorted photos of everyday life at Marion High School scattered amongst the pages of the 1955 yearbook are all of white students. There are only a handful of blacks in the pictures, usually in the athletic section. The school mascot, the Giant, was white, as was the homecoming queen and her court of twelve. The student council, all forty of them, are white. And the same holds for the National Honor Society, the Debate Club, the Drama Club, and, of course, the staff for the yearbook and the school newspaper. There was one black student in the marching band and one in the Bookworm Club, but no African Americans in the Science,

Latin, or Spanish clubs or the fifty-member Advanced Chorus.

The faculty was all white as was the school board, administration, and coaching staff. It becomes quickly apparent that blacks had limited access to many of the activities of the school. Only in athletics (girls' and boys') and two or three other minor organizations did there appear to be any mixing of the races. The Booster Club that cheered on the athletic teams was one. But the cheerleaders were all white and remained so for at least another thirty years. Even in athletics, while blacks are represented on the football, basketball, and track teams, the tennis, golf, and wrestling teams are all white.

The yearbook closes with photographs of the students by their classes—mixed, finally, due to traditional alphabetical listing. The class officers, though, are all white. Student leadership, not only in Marion, but also in most other places, even today, has yet to change very much.

* * *

While the Archey brothers lived and attended school in Marion, the divisions by race were both formal and informal. One of the formal separations was the segregation of the Matter Park Swimming Pool. Phil Matter, a well-to-do city father, had provided several acres of land for a public park on the north side of Marion along the banks of the Mississinewa River. It contained a small amusement park and zoo, picnic tables, tennis and horseshoe courts, a softball field, a band shell, and a museum full of artifacts from the county's history. Also within this park had been built a large swimming pool—for whites only.

Black children who wished to swim had to travel to a segregated pool in Anderson, a city thirty-five miles south of Marion. Don Hawkins was a veteran of World War II and an excellent athlete and swimmer. Chartering a dilapidated bus, he picked up black youth at the African American churches and took them on the hour-long drive. During these hot, humid summer days in Indiana, the cool blue water of the Matter Park Pool may as well have been the Pacific Ocean in terms of access for black children in the community.

In the midst of the *Brown* decision, the status quo of the Matter Park pool came under fire. Oatess and Tom, along with their good friend Don Ward, figuratively and literally "tested the waters" of the city's race code. An attorney and others from the local NAACP branch witnessed these routine denials of what today would be considered a basic right. And in 1954 the issue became "exactly whose right was it to use the swimming pool?" The history of the desegregation of the Matter Park Pool is one of national organizations and issues playing out in a local community. The NAACP and the Urban League—two organizations with different roots and missions—had local chapters in Marion. Both organizations worked together to fight the segregated swimming pool.

The NAACP had been founded in 1905 with the purpose of achieving political equality and civil rights. Emerging from the ideas and ideals of W. E. B. DuBois, the NAACP was the foremost

organization supporting black rights in a racist and segregated society. The National Urban League came into being five years later, in 1910. While mainly a black organization at its roots, the membership was a mix of blacks and whites, with whites often in

W. E. B. DuBois, scholar and civil rights pioneer.

leadership positions. The National Urban League became quite effective during the 1940s, when many blacks left behind menial, low-paying agricultural work in the South for the higher-paying industrial jobs in the cities of the North. The Urban League supported the transition these black citizens were making to seek a better economic life.

Inactive in Marion since before World War II, the local NAACP chapter had obtained a new charter in the city in 1954. Engaged in its historical mission of economic development, the National Urban League had been effectively operating in Marion since 1941. It was especially active in the 1950s, when it pressed General Motors, which had just opened its large Fisher Body plant in west Marion, to employ blacks. The Marion Urban League also supported Hawkins's summer swimming project that transported the black youth of Marion to Anderson.

To some, this action by the Urban League was seen as tacit support for the status quo of keeping blacks out of the Matter Park Pool. Others, however, viewed this action by the Urban League as a pointed embarrassment to the community, showing the prejudice and small-mindedness of the city leaders on the issue of race.

Additional community organizations joined the Marion Urban League in its fight against the segregated swimming pool. They viewed the Matter Park Pool question as comparable to any of the post-*Plessy v. Ferguson* "separate but equal" cases. The Marion City Park Board floated the idea of building another swimming pool. This mirrored the actions of other states that contemplated the building of separate facilities for blacks rather than having to integrate. Working in tandem, the NAACP and the Marion Urban League challenged the park board in behind-the-scenes negotiations. Openly, they continued to test the system by sending Oatess, Tom, and other blacks to the pool to gain admittance.

When these efforts failed, the NAACP filed suit in the U.S. District Court of Northern Indiana to integrate the Matter Park Swimming Pool. The decision came down in July 1954, just two months after the *Brown* decision. The federal court in Indiana echoed its Supreme Court brethrens' conclusion. The ruling, based on the Fourteenth Amendment to the U.S. Constitution, read in part that all persons would have "the full use and enjoyment of the Matter Park Swimming Pool." As was fitting, Don Hawkins became the first person of color to break the surface of the pool's water while breaking the color line at the same time.

Along with their black friends, the Archey brothers became frequent visitors to the once forbidden pool. Unfortunately, many whites decided to stay away. Martin Luther King Jr. had said that the law could not make whites love blacks. And it was true with this decision by the courts. The law had spoken, but a good number of Marion citizens did not feel compelled to follow the moral principle on which it was based.

Implementation of the *Brown* decision moved at a painfully slow pace across the nation. In some southern states, politicians and citizens did all they could to defy and disobey the court's ruling. In Virginia, for example, private schools were opened and public schools shut down. This forced black children to leave their homes and live with relatives in other towns in order to attend school. And while never taken to that extent, implementation of the spirit of the *Brown* case was ponderous at times in Marion. Following the idea of integration to its logical conclusion meant an end to separateness of black and white students *and* black and white teachers. The Marion High School of the 1950s that Tom and Oatess attended had no black teachers. In fact, it had never had a black teacher. But one day it would.

5

Being a Marion Giant

The 1930 lynchings were a constant strain on Oatess Archey and other blacks in Marion. Four years earlier, however, the community had come together on the same spot to celebrate. In March 1926 the Marion High School basketball team had won the state championship. Driving home on that cold night, the team had been greeted back home by an enthusiastic crowd that had started a huge bonfire on the south side of the courthouse square. The heat became so extreme that it scorched and cracked the cement sidewalk and steps, making it necessary for the city to replace them.

This team, coupled with the growing Hoosier fanaticism surrounding this emerging sport, had a powerful effect on aspiring athletes in Marion. Thirty, forty, even fifty years after this high school team became state champions, the names of the players were as familiar in Marion as any current-day celebrities. Two novels, written by Harold Sherman in 1926 and 1927, were loosely based on the Marion Giants. Books such as Sherman's were written for young boys to exemplify action, good sportsmanship, and adventure.

The actual Marion team became known as the Giants due to the fact that they had the first "big man" in the sport—six foot, seven inch Charles "Stretch" Murphy. But one tall kid alone could not make the team a winner. Murphy had help. His teammate, Robert Chapman, another talented big man, stood six feet, five inches tall. (The other three starters were Everett Chapman, Glen Overman, and Carl Kilgore.) Robert Chapman would go on to play for the University of Michigan, while Murphy attended Purdue University. Both Chapman and Murphy won All-American honors in college.

The first Indiana state high school basketball tournament was played in 1911. Crawfordsville won the game over Lebanon by a score of 24–17. Although the Indiana High School Athletic Association had been in existence since 1903, it had no real regulatory power over the state's sports until 1916, when Arthur Trester was named its commissioner. Trester gave state high school sports its structure, meted out punishments, and ran the association from his office in the Circle Tower in downtown Indianapolis. In 1925 Trester invited Dr. James Naismith, inventor of the game, to the state tournament. Naismith, part of a crowd of fifteen thousand people, was amazed that the game had grown from his original peach baskets on the wall of a gym to the "revelation" he observed in Indianapolis.

Robert and Helen Lynd wrote about Muncie, Indiana, in their 1929 book *Middletown: A Study in Contemporary American Culture*. In the book they considered "basket-ball" as "all pervasive as football in college" and stated that the teams "dominated the life of the school." Citizens unable to secure tickets to tournament games stood in the street and cheered a scoreboard that relayed the score from

Oatess Archey's senior photo.

inside the gymnasium. Classes were canceled during tournaments, but not before cheering, songs, and even prayers took place in pep rallies.

Although part of the overall high school facility, gymnasiums are not primarily academic in nature. They are places where the community showcases its basketball talent ten to twelve nights a year. Of the twelve largest gymnasiums in the United States today, ten of them are in Indiana. This state is where basketball has always been king, and where the game matters most.

The game described by the Lynds took on an even more special aura in Marion. Due to its history and its importance to city leaders, students, and fans, basketball players at the school were treated as heroes. In Marion these Giants hearkened back to the days of the Roman Empire. They even played their games in a place called the Coliseum. Built in 1926, the Memorial Coliseum replaced the team's previous venue—a small gymnasium above city hall and the police station. Competing in an old gymnasium would not do for what the community hoped would be a dynasty for future Giant teams. The new gym could seat 5,500 fans—an amazing number for that time.

A brief footnote can be added to these early days of the Marion Giants. Ovid Casey—Oatess's future father-in-law—became Marion's first African American boys' basketball player when he made the varsity team for the 1928–29 season. (A cousin of Oatess's, Ed Pettiford, became the first African American to play in the county as a member of the Fairmount High School team in 1927.) Playing center and forward, Ovid led the Giants to a berth among the final sixteen teams in the 1931 state tournament

* * *

Every kid who ever bounced a basketball and took shots at the many goals in town wanted to be a Marion Giant. One of the uniforms worn by the 1926 championship team was displayed in the small museum

41

Marion High School yearbook
photographs of Archey's sports career.

located in Matter Park. I gazed at that jersey and trunks for an inordinate amount of time. I also went to the public library and inconvenienced the librarian to examine the copy of the 1926 Cactus, the name of Marion High School yearbooks. These yearbooks were kept locked in glass bookcases in the Indiana Room. I now own my own copy. There were only two or three photographs of the team and their coach, Eugene Thomas. A small, powerfully built man, Thomas had a full head of thick curly hair resembling that of Harry Houdini. There were no blacks playing on this team.

A man who worked at my father's service station had been at that 1926 championship game. Half the building contained the temporary basketball floor and seats, while the other half housed fans without seats. Twice as many tickets as seats had been sold and roughly half the crowd had to wait for someone to leave to slip into an empty seat.

At that time, a jump ball was held at center court after each basket. I was told how "Stretch" Murphy always controlled the jump balls, giving the Giants a tremendous advantage. Teammate Bob Chapman was equal to Murphy in ability and only two inches shorter. Carl Kilgore was the floor guard and another Chapman—Everett—used to squint at the basket before letting his usually accurate shot fly. Shots at the basket were two-handed flings or underhanded tosses. The day of the one-handed jump shot was yet to come.

The game at that time was played in the backcourt, with no ten-second rule requiring a player to advance the ball toward the basket. The guard would wait for a player to break toward the basket and then fling a pass toward him. When such plays did not go well, a timeout would be called. But the players were not allowed to huddle with their coach. They were required to stay on the floor and talk things over among themselves. Murphy, the Giant captain, brought his teammates together by raising his hand high above his head, waving it for the players to gather around

43

him. The other piece of trivia that my coworker related to me was that before the start of each game, Coach Thomas passed out a stick of Beechnut Peppermint gum to each player and then shook hands with them.

Better than hearing about this legendary team or gazing at its fading photographs in the school annual was to actually see one of these legends. I went to school with the son of Bob Chapman. With pride he would tell how his father had scored the most points in the championship game and how he still had pieces of the net from that tournament. My friend's older brother later taught in the Marion school system, and I also knew him. These first Giants provided the motivation for players, fans, and coaches in the years that followed.

* * *

Oatess became a Marion Giant in his own right. First playing baseball, he briefly considered his brother's sport, cross country, under Coach Ray Sears. Marion was fortunate to have a coach of Sears's caliber on the staff. A graduate of Butler University, Sears had held the world indoor two-mile record. But running the rugged two-mile cross-country course did not appeal to Oatess. To play basketball though, an athlete had to participate in a fall sport. So Oatess eventually turned to football. In fact, Oatess became a three-sport letterman—football, basketball, and track. Although he won all-state honors in football and started on Coach Woody Weir's basketball team, his strongest performance came in track's high and low hurdles.

Weir had a profound impact on Oatess. Weir had been a three-year starter at Indiana University and then an assistant coach at Stanford University, where that team won the national championship. He then came to Marion in the mid-1940s. Weir was a technician of the sport. He instructed his players on exactly where to be on the court offensively and defensively, what type of pass to use in different situations, and how to make one-on-one moves against an opponent. He even directed them on how to position the ball as they attempted a jump shot.

In some ways Weir was the precursor to the energetic, activist coaches of recent times. He sometimes jumped from his seat, leapt over the bench, and confronted referees about questionable calls. Weir would peel himself out of his sport jacket and then go right back into the sleeves in one fluid movement. Norm Jones, one of Oatess's teammates, tells of being struck in the eye by the button on the coach's suit coat during one such frenzied outburst by Weir.

Weir's flamboyant coaching style overshadowed the technician in him. He could chew a player out one minute with humiliating remarks such as, "How can you let a little guy do that to you?" At other times, his discipline and approach to the game bordered on harassment. Out late one night, Jones had wrecked his car on an icy road. Although Jones was unhurt, the accident upset Weir in that one of his players could have been injured. The next practice Weir worked Jones over in the lane with elbows and offensive charges supposedly "demonstrating" defense to the rest of the team. Weir was the boss and a high schooler's carelessness was not going to cost the coach a win—not if he could help it.

Jones also tells of Weir catching two players smoking. He ordered them to run in front of his car for several miles, threatening at times to run them over. The two players thought this was their punishment for the forbidden act of smoking. But when Weir got them back to the Coliseum, he kicked them both off the team. Jones correctly points out that such tactics today would land a coach in jail or on the wrong end of a lawsuit.

Indiana basketball throughout most of the twentieth century was played without distinction to size of the school. Today almost all states divide schools according to their enrollment and have them play among schools in classes. Indiana has that system today. But when Oatess played basketball, the smallest school could face the largest school in the all-important state tournament held in the month of March. The state tourney was based on a four-week, four-tiered arrangement. Teams competed the first weekend in the sectionals that whittled the more than four hundred high schools in the state down to sixty-four teams. The two-game regionals the following Saturday reduced the number to sixteen teams. Two games at four sites across the state—known as the semistate—left four teams to journey to Indianapolis for the state finals.

Weir had taken his 1947 Marion Giants to the final four, but was defeated 59–50 by Terre Haute Garfield. Three years later, Weir came close again to matching the success of the legendary 1926 Marion Giant team. Led by the talented Pat Klein, the 1950 team again made it to the final four, but in a controversial call went down to defeat by one point in the afternoon game to Madison. The referee had called interference with the net on a last-second shot taken by Jim Barley, giving Marion a one-point lead. The official, however, later changed his call, giving Madison the win. Klein did receive the Trester Mental Attitude Award and was named Indiana's Mr. Basketball.

When his turn came, Oatess played on the Marion basketball team in Memorial Coliseum. Even the floor of Memorial Coliseum was special. The wood was kept highly glossed to a golden color and the lanes were painted deep purple—one of the two school colors, with the other being gold. A large letter *M* was in the center of the court. Local radio station WBAT broadcast the games from an organ-loft perch at one end of the court. Former all-state Marion Giant star Bill Fowler, from the 1940 team, performed the play-by-play announcing.

The basketball teams that Oatess played on during his high school years struggled. In fact, they never got beyond the sectionals, beaten his senior year in the Memorial Coliseum by Fairmount High School, also located in Grant County. At that time, Indiana high school rules called for a "sudden death" after two overtimes. This meant the first team to score after the two overtimes would be the winner. Oatess remembers watching the shot by Fairmount going through the net and the Giants' season, and his basketball career, both coming to an end.

Indiana had integrated schools, for those few blacks who attended, until the 1920s. The first black student to play on a state championship team was Dave DeJernett in 1930. From the town of Washington in southern Indiana, DeJernett played center. A death threat aimed at DeJernett was sent to the school during a previous tournament. It was signed by the Ku Klux Klan. After much discussion, his father let DeJernett play, but the senior DeJernett carried a pistol to the game in Vincennes. There was no violence. Later in the tournament, DeJernett led all scorers in the state championship game. His team beat Muncie Central by eleven points—the same number of points DeJernett scored.

The Ku Klux Klan dominated much of Indiana politics in the 1920s, including the Indianapolis school board. Attempting to curtail school integration in the city, the board passed zoning ordinances to control where blacks could go to school. In 1927 the Indianapolis school system built and opened an all-black high school named Crispus Attucks. Attucks, a black man, had escaped slavery as a youth only to be shot by the British in 1770 during the Boston Massacre. Larger Indiana cities such as Evansville and Gary followed suit with all-black schools. Attucks High School had a highly educated faculty due to the fact that many of the teachers held doctoral degrees. Excluded from teaching in white colleges, they often found positions in high school classrooms. During World War II strict adherence to zoning laws was eased and several high schools in the capital city allowed blacks to attend. The city's largest high school, Arsenal Technical High School, had a few blacks on its teams.

In 1948 Ray Crowe became an assistant basketball coach at

TOP: Crispus Attucks High School in Indianapolis. ABOVE: Attucks coach Ray Crowe. RIGHT: Indiana high school basketball legend Oscar Robertson.

Attucks. Two years later, Crowe took over as head coach. In his first few years Crowe followed a nonaggressive style of coaching—never challenging questionable calls or running up the score on clearly inferior opponents. Eventually, Crowe had his fill of biased officiating. He made sure the scores of the games were beyond the control of game-deciding calls being made by white referees. In 1955 Attucks became the first all-black school to win the state basketball title.

Men in striped shirts were not the only barriers a black athlete might confront in pursuing his sport. It was said that Branch McCracken, longtime head coach of the Indiana University Hoosiers basketball team, would only play one black player at a time. There was an unspoken rule some coaches went by in terms of how many blacks they would play—"Put one in the game when you are at home, two when you are on the road, and all five when you're down fourteen at half-time."

As in most of Oatess's life, racial issues were in transition. The post-World War II era had its own special problems. The decade from 1945 to 1955—the year Oatess graduated from high school—saw the integration of the armed forces and an upset presidential election win by Harry Truman. In 1948 Truman prevailed over three opponents, one of whom was Strom Thurmond, a rabid segregationist running on the Dixiecrat ticket. As Oatess moved through the Marion school system, another young black man was emerging on a parallel track in Indianapolis.

Oscar Robertson was a year younger than Oatess and would go on to make his mark in basketball at the high school, college, and professional ranks. There were similarities between the two young men. Growing up they had both played imaginary games in their backyards. Their mothers were gifted singers of gospel music and both families attended African Methodist Episcopal churches. In addition, their fathers preached the value of education and hard work. Robertson's family had moved north to Indiana via Tennessee, while one branch of Oatess's family had arrived through Tennessee and Kentucky. Both centered their activities on family and church. Robertson wrote, "In Indianapolis, basketball was the emperor of them all. Guys played from sunup to sundown." It was the same in Marion.

This issue of race, though, would be framed differently for Robertson in Indianapolis. In his autobiography, Robertson tells how his family was keenly aware of Ku Klux Klan activity in Indiana. He tells of driving by signs in the state that read "N _ _ _ _ _, Don't Let The Sun Set On You Here!" and seeing handbills passed out to whites that asked "Do You Want A N _ _ _ _ _ For A Neighbor?" And while the National Association for the Advancement of Colored People had successfully fought city zoning segregation laws, blacks were still forced to abide by curfew laws not applicable to whites. The young Robertson remembers seeing very few whites as he grew up in the black ghettos of the capital city.

While race and politics were playing themselves out on the national stage, these issues were also reflected on the local level in the cities and towns across 1950s America. In Marion the race issue became more personalized than the deeply held racism of a large urban city such as Indianapolis. During this time a white Marion High School student became pregnant and it was rumored that a star athlete, who was black, might be the father. One observer has stated that "it was the worst thing since the lynching."

City leaders believed the females paid undue attention to black athletes. Some of these citizens thought it might be a good idea to not let black males have such a high public profile. (In truth, being an athlete, regardless of race, both then and now, brings with it popularity and accolades from high school to the professional ranks.) Blacks could participate—winning, after all, was also a community value. But their visibility would be severely restricted, thereby curtailing the stereotypical gravitational pull black males allegedly generated on white females.

The unspoken guidelines limiting the playing time of black athletes affected both Tom and Oatess, especially in basketball. Blacks could play, but "not too many of them and not too much," one observer has noted. Tom, who graduated in 1953, played basketball as a Marion Giant, but according to Oatess, "it was tough on him." Oatess also started, but his role on the court would be narrowly confined. Players who scored points were the stars. So Oatess became the Dennis Rodman for his team. He rebounded and fed the ball to the white players, who did the majority of the shooting and scoring. If Oatess or any of the other blacks scored too many points, they found their playing time limited. Apparently, the community deemed the cost of having another black star too costly.

There is little doubt that Woody Weir was an outstanding coach. In 1975 he was inducted into the Indiana Basketball Hall of Fame. But clearly Weir was caught between community expectations to win and keeping black participation at a minimum. On road trips the team would stop for a pregame meal. Under the guise of finding out if the restaurant had enough room, coaches actually inquired as to whether the establishment served blacks. A number of them did not. In the late 1940s on overnight road trips to southern Indiana, black players would stay with black families "on the other side of the tracks," while the coaches and white players stayed in hotels. In Marion in the early 1960s, the Boston Celtics played an exhibition game at the Catholic high school gym. But the team was not allowed to eat at the Miller Supper Club, Marion's premier restaurant. A number of their players, including all-star Bill Russell, were black.

Weir seems to have undertaken some segregation on his own. During the 1955 sectional tournament held in Marion, he decided to keep the team together for meals and lodging. The Spencer Hotel, a six-story edifice that sat on the southeast corner of the city square, was segregated. So Weir bunked his basketball team at his own home, a large two-story frame house near the high school. Weir told the players to pick a buddy and then assigned them in pairs to a room. But before the three black players, Tom Nukes, David Pettiford, and Oatess Archey, could pick their friends—some of whom were white—the coach took them to the attic to sleep. While holding Weir in high esteem as a coach, the episode left resentment in these young men for years.

Weir had come close, but he could never bring home the big prize—the state championship. It was said that due to the fact he could never accomplish this singular feat, he lost his job. His coaching career came to an end. Not the administrative type, a role where many coaches finished their careers in education, Weir decided to teach physical education to elementary students. In addition, he built a basketball feeder system in these schools that would reap benefits for his high school coaching successors years later. But in the years immediately after he stepped down as coach, Weir would duck down an alley in embarrassment. He did not wish to face the fans who had at one time cheered him and his team on Friday and Saturday nights.

* * *

After his coaching years at the helm of the Marion Giants, Woody Weir would be my elementary school physical education teacher. In the late 1950s physical education was taught in the high schools and junior high schools. But rarely was physical education taught to elementary students. There was recess after all. Most school administrators thought that seemed enough exercise for youngsters. How Weir became an elementary physical education teacher is unclear. But as with anything he undertook, Weir threw himself into the job with energy and expertise.

Since few, if any, of the elementary schools had gyms, when the Indiana weather turned cold, Weir had to be creative. I remember him putting mats for tumbling workouts on the small stairway landings and even in the hallways at Horace Mann Elementary. He would joke with students and seemed jovial to most of us. We never saw the competitive, no-nonsense coach that Oatess and his teammates had experienced. I still remember him calling kids nicknames, including me. Noticing my tall height in fourth grade, one day he said to me, "Come on high-pockets, you can turn a summersault better than that." Whatever his shortcomings, Weir was a professional. He moved on after his coaching days and made a difference in the lives of thousands of Marion students.

6

On Becoming a Champion

Being first. Being a champion. Competition, rather than cooperation, is built into the formal and informal play, sport, and recreation of most youth. Whether on asphalt-covered playgrounds in the city or grassy rural fields, foot races were daily rituals when Oatess Archey was a schoolboy. As kids can quickly identify who is the best reader or speller, they can also identify the best athletes.

When the basketball season ends in Indiana—by early March for most schools and by the end of March for the final four schools in the state tournament—attention turns to the spring sports of golf, baseball, and track. In the days of the 1950s this meant boys' golf, baseball, and track. Federal legislation known as Title IX, which called for increased gender equity for student athletes, would not emerge until the 1970s. At Marion High School the Girls Athletic Association undertook the occasional inter-city games for some events. But for the most part, competitive sports were for the world of males, not females.

In his entire athletic career Oatess always sought for a way to be first. This was especially true in track and field, as he looked for a way to use his talents to the best of his abilities. Although he had excellent speed, he was not the fastest sprinter on the team. His brother Tom had been a long-distance runner, but that did not appeal to him and he did not think he could be competitive. He gave the high jump and pole vault a try, but again they did not seem the right fit for him. Then he noticed one of his cousins practicing on the hurdles. Maybe that event would be the one for him. With above average speed, agility, and a quick step, the hurdles seemed a perfect match for Oatess's talents.

Oatess took two hurdles home to practice on during the summers. He set them up along the side of his house, spacing the hurdles the appropriate number of feet apart to get the steps between them down perfect. The Archey family had a dog named Sport. Since most of the other kids in the neighborhood were swimming and playing baseball (and who would want to run, let alone run hurdles, in the humid Indiana summer heat), Oatess "challenged" Sport to train with him. He got Sport on the line, crouched into his starting position, and then yelled, "Go!" Working on his technique, his steps, and his style, Oatess ran his hurdles, getting faster and faster each day.

Oatess ran both the high and low hurdles, plus a leg on the 880-yard relay team. Sometimes he also competed in the high jump. His

Archey wins the 1955 state championship in the high hurdles, setting a record that remained unbroken for the next seven years.

specialty, however, became the 120-yard high hurdles. Each of the ten high hurdles spaced over the length of the course were thirty-nine inches high. The sport is unique. It is by nature based on an athlete's ability to maintain what has been called "an efficiency of interruption" while having a high rate of horizontal velocity. Synchronizing the leg, arm, and body is essential. Coordination of front leg, trailing leg, hand motion, and hip rotation are also all critical for success. Oatess learned to lean his body forward as he drove into each of the hurdles, making three sprinting strides before clearing the next barrier.

Today the hurdles are made of metal and weighted on L-shaped legs with eight pounds of resistance. In Oatess's day they were made of wood and less forgiving should a hurdler hit one. Clearing them as closely as possible to save time, while maintaining a rhythm, made the event more complex and challenging than is apparent from the stands. For Oatess, he and the hurdle were an immediate match. With his ability to go over a hurdle and not knock a dime off the top of it, the event almost seemed invented for his talents. His style was fluid as he

The photograph that appeared in the Marion Leader-Tribune *of Archey winning the state championship in the high hurdles.*

pushed and drove over the hurdles. Right heel over the hurdle with the left forearm in front of forehead—it is a running motion, not a jump. Muscles in the upper leg and hip are used and flexibility, coordination, and position all mesh into the pattern. All athletes need to think, but hurdlers need to think more.

Combining all of these elements and getting to the finish line first was what Oatess excelled at when running the hurdles. He had speed—anyone who had watched him play football or basketball could attest to that. But what about getting over the ten hurdles, the high hurdles, spaced over 120 yards on a cinder track? Again, Oatess had mastered this complicated task. A hurdle, after all, is a barrier. And Oatess always had barriers to overcome in his life. The point, as Marion Giant track coach Mike Byelene had simply but profoundly stated, was to "go over all the hurdles." And as with most barriers in life, there were special ways to go over them. But one went over the hurdles, never around them.

One way to accomplish the task quickly was to get over the hurdle with minimal daylight between the competitor's leg and the top slat that was usually painted with diagonal markings of black and white. Oatess could handle these three-foot, three-inch wooden frames with dispatch. Just as in practice at home, he had the knack of going over a hurdle and not disturbing that thin dime sitting atop it. The closer one could get to the hurdle, the quicker the time. It was all about dimes and times.

In 1955 Indianapolis was the focal point for sports in the state, as it served as the home for the famed Indianapolis Motor Speedway and such large arenas of that day as Butler Fieldhouse (later renamed Hinkle Fieldhouse in honor of the institution's longtime coach, Tony Hinkle) and the Coliseum on the Indiana State Fairgrounds. In addition, the city had a triple-A professional baseball team, one step below the major leagues, that played in a ballpark on Sixteenth Street called Victory Field. The high school state baseball championships were played on this field, and the state basketball and track championships were also held in Indianapolis.

As in basketball, making it to the state finals was the epitome for each track-and-field athlete. The Butler Fieldhouse was the hallowed hall for Indiana high school basketball. The same glamour held true for the terraced and manicured track-and-field facility of Indianapolis Arsenal Technical High School, then the largest high school in the state. The competing athletes included sprinters, distance runners, high jumpers and broad jumpers, shot putters, pole-vaulters, and of course, high and low hurdlers.

As the track season wound down for Oatess in May 1955, Marion was a mix of both the familiar and contemporary. Newspaper readers in Marion could find grocery store advertisements for Kellogg's Corn Flakes that sold for twenty-seven cents a box, three bars of soap could be purchased for the same price, and a one-pound can of beans went for a dime. On the comic page *Blondie* and *Mutt and Jeff* were to be found up to their usual antics. The front page that May reported that tests for the Salk polio vaccine were being put on hold for first and second graders pending medical reports as to its safety. During that month driver Bill Vukovich was killed on Memorial Day in a violent crash on the backstretch of the Indianapolis Motor Speedway. He was leading in his attempt to win his third 500-mile race in a row.

An editorial on June 2, the day after the state finals in track and field, addressed the year-old *Brown v. Board of Education* case, commenting on the lack of cooperation in the South. The probable need for more court cases, due to the absence of a time line to hold school districts accountable, was suggested. (The city's own problem with court ordered desegregation of its public swimming pool the year before was not mentioned.) And on Mother's Day that May, thirteen women were profiled in the local newspaper as exemplary role models. Oatess's mother, Orpha, was not one of those selected. But then all thirteen women selected were white.

Oatess had had a good track season that spring of 1955. He usually won the high and low hurdles and in one meet tied for first in the high jump, not even his main sport. Marion was a member of one of the most competitive high school athletic conferences in Indiana. The North Central Conference included high schools that were, for the most part, traditional Midwest automotive factory communities—Muncie, Lafayette, Kokomo, New Castle, Logansport, Frankfort, and Marion. Oatess had dominated the various meets and relays during the spring of 1955, but once or twice hurdlers from Muncie Central had beaten him. The Muncie hurdlers were Dick Steelwagon, Bob Odem (a future state champion), and John Casterlow. Oatess's best time all season long for the high hurdles had been 14.7 seconds.

Oatess had made it through the sectional and regional qualifying rounds on the road to the state finals, but his fortunes looked bleak this early summer day in Indianapolis. The fifty-second annual State Track and Field Meet, held on June 1, a Wednesday, had been postponed from the previous Saturday due to severe storms in the capital city. As a result of this postponement, Oatess had not run in ten days, although he had matched his season best time of 14.7 in the regional track meet on May 20. This was a record for that regional and the third time that season he had set that mark. He was a tenth of a second off the state record of 14.6 seconds. But then, on this special day in Indianapolis, a nagging back pain was making it difficult for him to move, let alone run.

Byelene was there to encourage Oatess. Byelene, who also coached football, had an athletic pedigree of his own. His high school football coach had been Paul Brown, who eventually became head coach and owner of the National Football League's Cleveland Browns. Byelene knew Oatess well and provided critical support at the state finals for his star hurdler.

Oatess had barely made the finals of the high hurdles in June with a mediocre fourth place finish in the preliminary heat. The back problem, later thought to be an unhealed football injury, had returned at this inopportune time to plague him. Eligible for the low hurdles, he "loafed" through that event according to the Associated Press, not qualifying for the finals. The Associated Press, though, was unaware that Oatess was suffering from an acute lower-back problem. It apparently believed that he had chosen to expend his strength and energy on his specialty, the high hurdles. Oatess sat, he stretched, and he talked to Byelene about the situation. Oatess had reached the pinnacle of his best sport, but now would it all be for naught?

As he would do throughout his life, Oatess turned to his religious faith for guidance. He sat under a cottonwood tree and softly uttered a prayer, "Let me run just one more race, just one more race." Then the call came for the finals in the high hurdles. Stepping into his lane, Oatess leaned, placed his fingers behind the white chalk starting line, stretched his legs back, and shook the cinders from his cleats. Bob Lee, longtime Marion newspaper sportswriter, filed this report in the next morning's sports section: "The meet produced five new records, one by a Marion athlete. Senior veteran Oatess Archey skimmed over the 120-yard high hurdles in 14.5 seconds to knock a tenth of a second off the three-year-old mark of Kokomo's Ken Toye. Archey . . . got over 'em in a hurry Wednesday and at the tape he was two yards in front of second-place John Ackerman of Jasper."

Inexplicably, Oatess's state record time was given the second headline of the article in his own hometown newspaper, the *Marion*

Leader-Tribune. Gary Froebel High School's team state championship was given the lead. Oatess's blue-ribbon achievement was not discussed until the fourth paragraph. "Froebel Wins State Meet; Archey Sets Hurdle Mark" read the banner headline. A striking photograph of Oatess, though, did accompany the article. He is captured in perfect form, elegantly extended over a hurdle, right leg under left arm with his left leg trailing—flat out, fleet, and clearly ahead of his trailing competition gliding to victory. With his win, and the efforts of four fellow Giant trackmen, Marion High School's team finished fifth in the state meet.

The day after his championship dash over the hurdles, Oatess was honored at the Marion High School's year-end award ceremony. He was selected the outstanding senior athlete. A standout in three sports—football, basketball, and track—his athletic ability, cooperation, and mental attitude were all considered in his selection for the award. Oatess was also given the trophy for his record-breaking state victory in the high hurdles in Indianapolis. His record in the high hurdles remained unbroken until 1962.

The individual nature of most track and field events made this victory for Oatess one he could personally cherish. He could and did compete successfully in team sports. But this singular state championship—in record time no less—placed Oatess in select company. He had overcome a potentially devastating injury to not only compete, but also prevail. As Byelene had admonished and urged his star athlete, "You have to go over all the hurdles." He had indeed gone over all of the hurdles that early June afternoon in Indianapolis and had gone over them as a champion.

7

Welcome Home

To most men and women, a hometown is a place where one can hope to feel welcome, comfortable, and for some even honored. A hometown, like a home, should be a place of security and familiarity. So when new teacher Oatess Archey decided to return to Marion, Indiana, after receiving his certification as a teacher, he had no reason to think his return would be anything but positive and hospitable. He had been a star athlete there and his friends and his family and his wife's family all lived there. The reality of Oatess's return, however, failed to live up to any of his dreams.

Marion, Indiana, in 1959—in spite of the conventional wisdom that said the North was more enlightened and racially integrated—was not a harmonious place where races mixed easily. Progress, however, could be pointed to on some fronts. This was especially true in comparison to such past episodes as cold-blooded shootings, lynchings, and disputes over basic issues as integrating public facilities. While blacks did hold jobs on the police and fire departments, the faculty of the city's schools remained an all-white domain. Oatess found that some people in Marion wished for it to remain so.

The expanding school-aged population, due to the baby boom years following World War II, had made education a primary concern.

Teaching had become a popular vocation for many in these postwar years and demand for teachers was high. Marion was no exception. One of the midwestern automotive centers, Marion, similar to Muncie, Anderson, and Kokomo, was a factory town that had grown to almost 40,000 citizens.

Oatess was ready to teach and to coach. The response he received to his interest in a teaching job was quick. The superintendent was a kindly, white-haired grandfatherly figure, but not a progressive administrator. He told the eager applicant that Marion had never had a "Negro" teacher in its white schools before. The term "colored" may have even been used. Exactness in language in matters of race was neither codified nor precise in 1959 and terms such as African American or black did not emerge until the late 1960s. While Indiana was one of the states that allowed segregation of the races in schools and public facilities, law did not mandate it. The all-black Crispus Attucks High School in Indianapolis and the black elementary schools Brownlee and D. A. Payne School in Marion demonstrated that this de facto segregation, pre- and post- *Brown v. the Board of Education,* occurred both north and south of the Mason-Dixon Line.

Oatess's brother Tom attempted to cross the color line as a teacher. Returning home with his teaching certificate and a degree from Grambling State University in 1957, he applied to be on the faculty of the Marion Community Schools. The answer was no. Tom then returned to Louisiana, but had no better luck in the city of Winnfield, Louisiana, a town near Shreveport. It was an all-black school, but school officials considered Tom a potential troublemaker due to the fact that he was from the North. Blocked from teaching, Tom worked laying sewer pipes until a friend was killed. After that he decided to quit. He then served a two-year stint in the army. Returning to civilian life, he again tried to find a teaching job. In an interview, the principal advised him not to say a word when interviewing with the superintendent. "You don't talk like a southern Negro. Only say 'yes' or 'no' and keep your mouth closed." The tactic worked. Tom began a distinguished career in teaching and administration, first in Catholic and then in public schools. He later earned his doctorate in education.

Oatess had offers for scholarships at several universities due to his accomplishments in track, football, and basketball. These scholarship offers came from such institutions as Indiana University, Tennessee State University, and Drake University, in addition to schools in Texas and Georgia. But he chose to attend the historically black Grambling College, founded in 1901 as the Colored Industrial and Agricultural School.

The Louisiana school followed the vocational model established for black higher education in the late 1800s by Booker T. Washington at his Tuskegee Institute. In stark contrast was the other black leader of the time W. E. B. DuBois. His approach to civil rights was much more confrontational. DuBois advocated blacks entering professional occupations. In contrast, Washington and many other leaders of historically black colleges preached against challenging segregation. His philosophy was based on his view that blacks needed to gain the vocational skills and knowledge necessary to succeed in a segregated society. Washington may not have agreed with the status quo any more than DuBois, but confronting whites publicly was not a method he chose to use.

First privately supported, what was to become Grambling State University became quasi-public in 1913. By then it had broadened its mechanical and agricultural focus to include training teachers. The school added the common term "normal" (meaning teacher education) to its name in 1928. At first, basically a two-year junior college, the institution inaugurated its first four-year programs soon after and graduated its first bachelors in education degrees in 1944. The institution became accredited in 1949 under its new name Grambling College.

When Oatess arrived at the college to join brother Tom in the fall of 1955, business and liberal arts programs had also been added. There were also new buildings from state funds to lessen the blatant inequity of facilities between black colleges and white colleges in the state of Louisiana. In Oatess's sophomore year, Grambling surpassed the two thousand mark in student enrollment and doubled that number a decade later.

Oatess had chosen to attend Grambling as a way to not only extend and expand his personal world beyond his midwestern roots, but also as a way to examine what it meant to be a black man in America. He had lived in an all-white neighborhood and attended a predominantly white high school. So he elected to enroll in an all-black college to discover what he might have missed in terms of his racial identity. Historically black colleges also produced graduates with strong leadership characteristics. The black professors frequently reminded their black students that they would be held to a higher standard. This was a theme the Archey brothers had heard often at home. They had to have the knowledge, skills, and dispositions to make them stand above their white counterparts. This provided them a competitive edge in the marketplace and in life.

Located in northern Louisiana, Grambling was small and much more rural than Marion, Indiana. Oatess and his parents made the journey to Louisiana by car on one occasion. The rest of the time, Oatess and Tom flew on commercial airlines or rode the train from Indiana to the Grambling campus. Traveling by train from north-central Indiana through Illinois and Missouri into Arkansas, the Archeys finally arrived in Louisiana. Journeys by car took them through

Kentucky and Tennessee, then into Arkansas and Louisiana. Those trips by automobile in the 1950s made clear what the Archey family already knew—they were living in a divided society. The four-lane interstate road system was just beginning under President Dwight D. Eisenhower's leadership. So the trip on two-lane highways was long, extremely hot in the early fall and late spring, and bitterly cold in winter.

The overnight accommodations were segregated, of course, as were most of the restaurants. Those restaurants that were not segregated required blacks to get their food from the back door. The same held true for restroom facilities. Oatess never forgot the embarrassment of waiting for his sister-in-law to use what passed for a toilet behind a country store in the South.

In June 1957 Oatess married his high school sweetheart, Barbara Jean Casey, who had graduated one year before Oatess. Her father's death a year following her graduation from high school dashed Barbara's hopes of attending college and becoming a nurse. Responsible for the care of both her mother and younger brother, she worked two years at a salary of ninety-four cents an hour at Hills Department Store, eventually making a dollar an hour. In September Oatess returned to Grambling to complete his last two years of college.

Oatess's career at Grambling on the track-and-field team was not what he had expected. As a freshman he placed seventh in the 110-meter high hurdles at a national meet in San Diego. He ran against Lee Calhoun and Hayes Jones, who both went on to run in the 1960 Rome Olympics. From that point on though, injuries plagued him. The competition varied and when he did perform well he was often overlooked coming from a small, relatively unknown school such as Grambling. He chose education as his major just like his brother Tom. He became certified to teach history, physical education, and health.

Upon his graduation, Barbara and Oatess began their new life together in their hometown of Marion.

The years of the late 1950s, as Oatess was attending Grambling, were a critical period in the history of civil rights in America. As a backlash against the *Brown v. Board of Education* decision, a number of southern states decided to reject the high court's opinion. Some white

Rosa Parks sits in the front of a bus in Montgomery, Alabama, after the U.S. Sepreme Court ruled segregation illegal on the city bus system on December 31, 1956.

parents removed their children from public school and enrolled them in private schools. In other communities the struggle against integration became more confrontational. In Arkansas, which is thirty miles north of Grambling, Governor Orville Faubus refused to allow Little Rock Central High School to enroll black students. After much hesitation, President Dwight D. Eisenhower enforced the law of the land, sending federal troops to ensure that nine black high school students received safe escort through angry mobs of whites.

The other major event of these years was the Montgomery, Alabama, bus boycott. Unwilling to give up her seat in the front of a bus for a white passenger, Rosa Parks challenged the state's segregation law and was arrested. This led Doctor Martin Luther King Jr. and other ministers to organize alternative ways for blacks to get to work rather than ride the buses. After many weeks and months, the bus company relented and blacks sat where they chose.

Now it was Oatess's turn to test the waters of integration and also attempt another hurdle in his life. A few other school districts in Indiana had broken the color line in terms of hiring black faculty. Oatess submitted his teaching application to the superintendent's office and was told that Marion was not ready to take the step of hiring a black teacher.

With that door seemingly shut, Oatess went to work in a Radio Corporation of America factory. He worked there only two weeks before being laid off during a summer shutdown. Oatess was then employed by General Motors. But again, after only three weeks, a GM strike closed the plant for a year. When this occurred, Oatess tried again with the Marion Community Schools and this time got a job as a custodian.

School Maintenance Superintendent Merle Rife encouraged Oatess to continue to push the central administration to hire him as a teacher.

But the school superintendent did not think it was the right time. It was a familiar refrain—"Marion wasn't ready yet." His brother Tom had heard it and now so did Oatess. Oatess was told, though, that if the time did come, he would be one of the first of his race to be considered. But who knew?

All honest work deserves respect. And all labor, including janitorial work, is important. Oatess was confronted with the dilemma between what he had been educated to do and what he was being permitted to do. It was difficult for Oatess to grasp that he was going to become a maintenance man for the Marion school system. At first Oatess was stunned. Then he was outraged. A custodian? A janitor? Such positions were nothing out of the ordinary for blacks or uneducated whites. But after four years of college, this new job appeared little more than an insult. Returning home he inwardly reflected on what it would mean to him personally to accept the job and said to himself, "Not in a million years." Quite a welcome home, he thought.

Oatess's wife, Barbara, had a different view of the school district's offer. Although never an appeaser, she had the ability to see not just tomorrow, but the day after tomorrow. The notion that skin color disqualified one from the teaching profession was as repugnant to Barbara as it was to Oatess. Yet even a giant of the civil rights movement, such as Thurgood Marshall, was a gradualist. After some mild persuasion, Barbara convinced Oatess that the custodian job offered at least a chance to get his foot in the door of the school district. Not much of a foot and even less of a door, Oatess may have thought. Again the phrase, "Welcome home," reverberated in his mind.

With the days of accolades and glory on the high school football field in the not too distant past, Oatess found himself again on his hometown's gridiron. This time, though, there were no cheers ringing in his ears. His first task as an employee of the Marion Community

Schools was to sweep out the dressing rooms, clean the restroom sinks and toilets, and pick up trash thrown under the bleachers from the previous Friday night football game. On game days, he lined the field with white chalk, marking every five yards and the end zones. He also poured cement, drove a tractor, and cut weeds. Of all these tasks, the most repulsive of all was spearing trash with a wooden stick with a sharp nail on the end. To this day Oatess finds the sight of this common tool revolting.

In September 1959 Oatess was doing his job on a warm Friday evening at a Marion Giant football game. A group of high school boys spit on him as he walked behind the south bleachers of Memorial Field. As he wiped the spittle from his face, he thought to himself that these boys who had yet to finish high school had just abused a university graduate. Oatess, who a brief four years before—helmeted and wearing the school's colors—had been cheered by adults and students alike for making a catch or scoring a touchdown. Now he was the target of obnoxious adolescent behavior. "Welcome home," he muttered again under his breath.

"I'm not going back," Oatess told Barbara at home that night. If one is not black and been treated in thoughtless and unfair ways, living on a daily basis with prejudice and discrimination, then it is difficult to place oneself in Oatess's shoes. He asked himself if he had merely been an entertainer for the white community as a high school athlete. Now that those days were over, who cared? Cleaning the toilets in the locker rooms added insult to mental injury. Again, Barbara quelled the unrest in Oatess's mind and heart. How they managed is difficult to understand. But they did and he returned to the job the next day. Oatess's trust in Barbara was complete and he endured a bit longer.

As the Indiana weather turned cooler that fall, the leaves began to change to red and orange. The weeks slowly passed. The once green grass on the football field turned khaki and was in need of mowing by Oatess less often. But the white lines every five yards and the lengths and width of the playing field still needed their weekly coat of chalk. Oatess pushed the lining machine across the ground still thinking, no doubt, "What am I doing here on a Friday morning?"

This thought and others ran through Oatess's mind, when a dark sedan pulled into the parking lot and the portly figure of the school superintendent emerged. He entered through the open gates of the stadium and walked toward Oatess. Superintendents were usually good politicians and so was this one. A quick, but friendly greeting from the dark-suited administrator was given. Meeting Oatess midfield, he quickly got to the point of his visit. "Would you still be interested in being in the classroom?" he asked. Interested? Although temporarily sidelined on his return home and his quest to become a teacher and a coach, just such thoughts had kept Oatess going as he did his mindless custodial chores day after day.

Oatess said that he was still interested in teaching. The superintendent told him to come to his office on Monday morning. The administration offices were located inside Memorial Coliseum— the building where the Marion Giants had taken the floor each season and where Oatess had played. Wearing a suit with a freshly ironed white shirt and neatly knotted necktie, Oatess entered the superintendent's office, his mind racing. Where would he be teaching? How did this position become available in the middle of October? Which building? Could it be Marion High School? Even one of the junior highs would be acceptable.

The superintendent's secretary formally greeted Oatess and had him sign a teaching contract. His starting salary was $4,200 a year. The secretary then took Oatess to see the superintendent, who smiled and

TOP: *The Grambling track team in 1956. Oatess is in the back row, second from left. His brother, Tom is on the far right of the second row.* LEFT: *Oatess uses a plastic model to explain the function of the heart to his students in health class.* RIGHT: *A 1965 faculty photo of Oatess at Jones Junior High School in Marion.*

invited him to take a seat. Maybe Barbara was right after all, thought Oatess, this may turn into something positive. It had taken time and patience, but now things were moving his way. The superintendent got right to the point. But Oatess's initial excitement over the weekend that had included calls to his relatives with what seemed to be good news was quickly dampened. It would not exactly be a teaching job and it would not exactly be his own classroom. "You see," the superintendent said, "we have this very nice fifth grade teacher—right next door here at Grant Elementary School—who is having some trouble keeping order in her classroom. She's a good person and can teach, but we need someone to help with discipline."

"Discipline" was the euphemism that meant keeping the students under control, making them behave, being an enforcer. This was not teaching. "Maybe I'd better get back out to the football field and finish cleaning the toilets and picking up the trash," thought Oatess. But he cautiously replied, "Okay, I'll take the job." He was directed to sit in the back of the room and deal with disruptive students. The job seemed to consist of barking out orders to unruly children such as "Stop it" or "Don't do that" or "Pick that paper up." The job might be considered closer to a bouncer or a sergeant at arms than an educator. "I went through fours years of college to do this?" Oatess thought to himself.

Oatess again returned home despondent. And again, Barbara bolstered his damaged pride. "What you did today is a step up from what you were doing yesterday," she told him.

"Barbara, I can't go back tomorrow and play policeman again," lamented a beleaguered Oatess the evening after his first day.

"You're a teacher, right?" she asked him.

"Of course I'm a teacher," he quickly replied.

"Help the students with their math, reading, and then take them out for recess," Barbara suggested. "See if the teacher will agree to your requests." Although she was right, it was not without deep reservations that Oatess returned to Grant School for his second day of work.

The offer to help was well received by the teacher. In fact, no sooner was it made by Oatess than a thud was heard as papers needing to be graded hit the top of his desk. Not as impressive or prestigious as being in the front of one's own classroom, but then again policemen did not grade papers. As the days passed, Oatess developed a bond with the students. They liked him and he liked them. He still had to play the role of "cop" on occasion, but that was all right for now. A mutual respect developed as Oatess's orientation to teaching was beginning. Although not a traditional path, he began to learn what the profession was about.

Oatess enjoyed assisting students with their math problems, grammar worksheets, and spelling lists. This time he did not debate the worth or value of his time on such tasks. Teachers graded papers, and now he was grading papers. Teachers helped students learn, and he was doing that too. In addition, Oatess took handicapped children to the YMCA for elementary swimming lessons.

The next step in Oatess's march toward full membership in the teaching profession came quite naturally. Oatess wanted to be a coach, so he asked the teacher if he could take the class out for recess. As winter set in, the other teachers wondered if Oatess would mind taking their students out for recess as well. Oatess knew this was just a crafty way for the teachers to escape playground duty, especially during the cold, Indiana winter. Playground duty was kind of coaching, so Oatess agreed.

The students of Grant Elementary School found Mr. Archey (Mr. Archey, which sounded like music to Oatess's ears) a vast improvement over their other teachers. Many teachers just stood around during the fifteen-minute recess time looking bored. Oatess knew all about games and competition and, best of all, he had been selected for just such physical activity.

Since Grant School sat next to Memorial Coliseum, the superintendent could observe Oatess working with the students by looking out his office window. Who knows what this veteran school administrator thought about issues of race and equity and professionalism or whether he thought about them at all. But it was clear this young black man connected with students. Maybe his talents were being wasted playing warden to misbehaving boys and girls and taking recess duty for the other teachers.

There was no doubt in Oatess's mind that there had to be other teaching positions available in the Marion school system. The post-World War II baby boom was at its height and the demand for teachers was high. But hiring the first black teacher might be too bold of a step for cautious school superintendents. It was often said that with school boards made up of seven members, superintendents only needed to know how to count to four—a majority—to be successful. This superintendent, though, decided to give Oatess a full-time teaching position the following year at a salary of $4,400. But it was not to be one of the better teaching assignments. The position required Oatess to drive each day between two schools. He taught elementary physical education a half day at McCulloch Junior High School, and then finished by teaching health and history classes at Martin Boots Junior High School. In spite of the travel and multiple class preparations, he was finally teaching full time.

Having one's own classroom, desk and chair, filing cabinets, and a place to store instructional materials was every teacher's goal, but this was not to be for Oatess. This was a split assignment. New teachers have traditionally been assigned the most difficult classrooms and in the least attractive settings. What were called "splits" would fall into this latter category. There were two kinds of split classes—one was where the teacher taught two grade levels in one room. The other type of split was between two schools. Neither one was easy for a teacher.

Except for bad weather and not having a home base from which to operate, the situation was acceptable to Oatess. And to top things off in 1961, he was going to coach. Martin Boots Junior High School was located between the Third Street and Fourth Street hills about five blocks west of downtown Marion. Many of the better basketball players had emerged from Horace Mann Elementary School, located next to Martin Boots. There were even basketball goals on both sides of the building. The gym had no seats, so games had to be played at other schools or at the Memorial Coliseum. But Oatess had himself a team—and quite a team it was. Best of all, he would get to keep the team for two consecutive years. The coach and his players enjoyed mutual success and respect.

How had Oatess managed to persevere through these obstacles and hurdles that appeared every step of the way? His minister had once said, "It's okay to get knocked down, as long as you don't get knocked out and you can look up and you can get up." True believer that he was, Oatess kept his faith and knew there would be a better tomorrow. His confidence and conviction paid off. Within four years he had a record of sixty-four wins and only seven losses as a junior high basketball coach.

* * *

The first impression was not that the teacher was black. (The acceptable term in 1961 was Negro, but most people in Marion used the word colored.) What surprised us was that we had a male teacher who specialized in physical education and coaching. After seven years of only female teachers, I was amazed to have a male teacher—several male teachers as a matter of fact. Oatess Archey was my physical education teacher.

Mr. Archey was out of the ordinary, and not just because he was black. He seemed to have it "all together," as we said at the time. The way he dressed, combed his hair, his organization, knowledge, authority—just the way he carried himself in general. And then, there was the way in which he talked. It was different from how the blacks we knew spoke. He had an almost neutral accent. He did not sound like a Hoosier, let alone a person of African American descent.

The son of my father's customer was my teacher and I was thrilled. The junior high school girls were allowed to use the small gym at Martin Boots. The boys walked two blocks down the Third Street hill to the Y Community Center or YMCA for classes. This edifice was a compromise in name and structure. Never really finished, it had partial rooms, much concrete that showed little or no paint, and veneer with exposed pipes. What looked like the outlines of future rooms were scattered throughout the building. The gym was fairly complete and there were two classrooms where health and social studies classes were taught.

At my elementary school, there had been no dressing room, only a small restroom with a single shower stall. But now we "dressed out," as Mr. Archey called it. There was almost a military bearing to it all, which continued when we lined up for attendance to make sure everyone had "dressed out" properly. This meant the Martin Boots T-shirt and shorts, white socks (dark or street socks were forbidden), tennis shoes, and, of course, a jockstrap. To assure that this last item of equipment was in place we would reach up through the bottom of our trunks, hook our thumb around the strap and pull down to show the line monitor and then snap it back into place—modest, efficient, and quick.

We would first march, do left and rights, pivoting on our shoes, and then some calisthenics to warm up. Class activities included dodgeball, kickball, tumbling, the trampoline, and some running. We never played basketball. Mr. Archey was not my basketball coach my first year of junior high school. I got lost on the second or third string B team for the rest of my seventh grade year.

It would be a Friday afternoon in late November just after lunch that another unforgettable moment occurred in my life in one of these YMCA makeshift classrooms. I was sitting in a social studies classroom working on a map of Indiana counties. Mr. Archey, who was in the gym teaching a class, stepped into the back of our classroom and told our teacher that he had just heard that President John F. Kennedy had been shot. The date was November 22, 1963.

Mr. Archey never "dressed out" himself, because he also taught health classes and he could not make multiple changes of clothes during the day's seven class periods. We knew he could play basketball—putting on his gym shoes one day, he touched the top of the painted box on the glass backboard. He also, at our prompting, admitted that he could dunk. And there was little doubt that he could run. He just looked fast.

I remember one spring day having a physical education class outside the school rather than at the YMCA. One of the guys who had heard that Mr. Archey had been a state champion hurdler asked him to go over one for us. I'm not sure exactly what we were doing, but I won't ever forget that there was a hurdle standing next to the building. "Come on Mr. Archey," the boy pleaded, "do a hurdle for us." Actually it did not take much encouragement from us. He placed the hurdle away from the building and then stood only three or four feet from it. Then, in a lightning fraction of a second, he "stepped" the hurdle.

It happened so quickly that we all shouted in unison "Do it again, do it again!" In his street clothes, Mr. Archey seemed to prance for a couple of steps in place and then, "zap"—over the hurdle in a dancing motion that made it seem there was no hurdle there at all. It was like magic. One *moment he was on one side of the hurdle and the next he was on the other side. If he could go over a hurdle in full-length pants with such speed and quickness, then it was no wonder he had been a state champion.*

Students are often surprised to see their teachers outside of school. They must think that teachers live at school—eat all their meals in the cafeteria, shower in the gym, sleep in their classrooms. Why else would students be so surprised to see them in grocery stores, driving their cars, or eating pizza with their families on Friday night? But observing teachers outside the school setting added a human dimension to a unique relationship.

Watching teachers was a full-time job for students. Not just in class, but what they did out of class. My buddies and I would go to football games and Mr. Archey would be there. Thinking about it now, we kids were probably a pain in the neck for him, but he would always talk to us. He drove a black Volkswagen Beetle and sometimes his wife Barbara and small son Eugene were with him.

While Mr. Archey was not the seventh grade basketball coach, he was our cross-country coach. The old, unwritten rule continued that to play basketball, you had to do something in the fall—either football or cross-country. Not really built for football, I chose cross-country. We practiced in the parking lot of the Memorial Coliseum and on a hill east of the building. Our meets were held on the grounds of the Veteran's Hospital in south Marion or near Matter Park on River Road.

* * *

While coaching was central to Oatess in his career, the majority of his day was spent in the classroom. Teaching six classes a day with one period for preparation is more difficult than many noneducators realize. Mr. Archey the teacher, rather than Mr. Archey the coach, taught physical education, health, and history at the junior high school level. He later shifted to the role of school counselor at the junior high school and then moved on to Marion High School as a health and driver's education teacher.

Oatess and Barbara became parents in 1961. Their first son was named Oatess Eugene Archey II and went by Eugene. Another son, Marlon Walton Archey, was born two years later. The boys attended football games and other sporting events with their parents.

The 1960s were a turbulent time of riots, demonstrations, and sit-ins. In the fall of 1968 this restlessness visited Marion High School. Oatess was the only black teacher in a school of 225 African American students and 2,475 white students. There was a fight in the cafeteria. The alleged causes ran the gamut from a small group of troublemakers causing mischief to racially motivated actions by both whites and blacks. It has even been suggested that white adults deliberately provoked the black students. By the time Oatess reached the cafeteria the trouble was over, but word spread that it had been a riot. Twenty years later there were eight black teachers and seven hundred fewer students. The system and the city itself continued to be more inclusive, with blacks having the top leadership roles on the school board, city council, city police department, and even a black superintendent of schools in the late 1990s.

During the 1960s new methods and ideas were being explored in the classrooms of America to make schooling more relevant to students. Oatess was always looking for new ways to make his classes more meaningful to his students. Matching the importance of physical education and health to his students' needs, Oatess tested various instructional approaches in his classroom.

One example was teaching acceptance of all types of diversity through his curriculum. For Oatess, race was but one example of diversity. Another was the stigma that was often placed on individuals who experienced problems in the area of mental health. Attempting to help students become more open to such individuals, one day Oatess planned a unique lesson. He approached one of his basketball players and asked him to role play in class the next day.

"How many people in here," Mr. Archey asked his class the next day, "consider Bob to be your friend?" Most of the students who knew Bob raised their hands. Mr. Archey then said, "I have talked to Bob and he told me I could share this with you. For two years Bob was in an institution for individuals that have mental problems. Now that you know that about Bob, how many of you still want to be friends with Bob?" A stunned class looked at Bob and Mr. Archey and then only one hand went up. A fellow basketball player who was black, Roger Clark, was the only student who still wanted to be Bob's friend. Mr. Archey then told the class that Bob had not been in a mental institution and that he and Bob had set up this role-playing scenario the day before. It was a lesson that stayed in the minds of his students regarding prejudice—prejudging a person on the basis of some attribute the person may have.

* * *

I never forgot that lesson because I was "Bob." I shared another distinctive experience with Mr. Archey, this time outside the classroom and athletics. Two teachers and two students, including Mr. Archey and me, played together in a band for the ninth grade year-end dance. Mr. Archey played drums and, as with most things, he was quite good. I am not sure how we found this out, or even how we put the onetime band together.

A classmate who played lead guitar joined me on keyboard and a science teacher was on rhythm guitar. We became "The Lotuses," the name of a British racing team popular in the 1960s at the Indianapolis Motor Speedway. Covering two or three songs by The Beatles, we played at the end of the evening. I remember that we practiced in my living room, and my mother talked a local music company into placing an organ in the gym for this brief concert. We were "one-night wonders," and the ten-minute stint we undertook was fun while it lasted. "Get a female singer and another guy or two and this band might go somewhere," the science teacher on guitar said at the end of the evening. He might have been right, but we will never know.

8

Coach

Although coaches must be blessed with players who have talent, talent at the junior high school level still calls for development. Basketball, as it was played in the 1960s, was different from the basketball of the 1920s and quite different from the game we know today. In the 1960s the game was dominated on both the college and professional levels by offensive stars.

Accordingly, younger players emulated these role models. Defense was mainly an exercise in the various zones to be employed, rather than in the way one guarded an opposing player. So it was shoot, shoot, shoot. One of the common phrases that players would use—in the gyms, on the playgrounds, in the back alleys—was "shoot, gun, you're loaded." It was all about shooting and scoring.

Coach Oatess Archey, although most of the players called him Mr. Archey, knew that it would take a more comprehensive approach for teams to be successful. And that meant not just "running and gunning." Passing, screening, blocking out, being in the right place at the right time, and effectively playing defense one-on-one, not just in a zone, were all needed. Offense was never left out, though, and under Oatess's tutelage, players were taught how to shoot the ball. For Oatess this meant getting the ball above your head—not throwing the ball at the

85

basket from the waist or even chest. In a competitive game, for shots to be successful, they had to be launched from the highest point possible. An improperly executed jump shot, one that was easy to block, had no chance of making it to the rim. Oatess, like John Wooden and other clever coaches, did most of his instruction during the daily practices. Trying to teach during a game did not work.

During the two seasons Oatess coached his first group of boys, the teams were highly successful. Players such as Doug Brown, Richie Keen, and John Sutter, mixed with Oatess's guidance and encouragement, were a recipe for success. Marion Community Schools had created, under the direction of former coach Woody Weir, a feeder system. Elementary schools had competitive teams that played other schools in the city. With almost ten elementary schools in the district, these fifth and sixth graders were able to develop just as Little League baseball players did during the summer.

What kind of coach was Oatess? Two of the best-known college coaches in recent years have been Dean Smith at the University of North Carolina and Bobby Knight at Indiana University. These men came after Oatess coached, but they are each representative of a distinct coaching philosophy. Smith was soft spoken, deliberate, thoughtful, and a gentleman. No one probably thought of Knight as a gentleman. Gruff, belligerent, frequently foulmouthed, Knight was known to yell at his players, yank at their jerseys, and once even tossed a chair the width of a court.

The community of Marion would probably not have accepted a screaming, aggressive coach who dealt with his players like Knight. They would have especially not accepted that kind of coaching behavior from a black man working mainly with white players. The Knight model was not the Archey model. It just did not fit his personality or his coaching philosophy. The Smith approach more closely matched that of Coach Archey. Therefore, the community supported Oatess. It was a different story, however, in other communities.

One such school was located within sixty miles of Marion. The city had undergone the demographic shift that many areas across the nation experienced during the 1950s and 1960s. The predominantly white middle class moved to the suburbs, leaving the city's urban center predominantly black. Along with the growth of suburban America came the building of new businesses, new churches, and new schools. Coach Archey took his junior high basketball team to play in one of these new suburban schools.

Refereeing is a thankless job and in every game most folks in the stands think they could do better than those wearing the striped shirts. On this night, however, the calls went beyond honest mistakes or missed views of plays. The whistles were blowing and they were not blowing for Coach Archey's team. At a timeout, one player complained, "Mr. Archey, it's not fair, they're cheating us!" Coach Archey calmly told his team, "Stick in there, you can still win." And they did. As the bus took the team back home that winter night, the players chattered about the unjust and questionable fouls and whether the referees were really counting out a full three seconds on lane violations. Coach Archey did not share his own thoughts on the game that evening until many years later. The calls were not to stop the team, but to block the success of the coach. The refs, the crowd, and the community could not stand to see a black man coach a mostly white team and win. "The '60s were tough," Oatess noted in an understated tone years afterwards.

This coach was the product of his own coach. While not modeling himself after his high school basketball coach in temperament and style—Woody Weir was more Knight than Smith—Oatess did replicate him in the area of tactics and strategy. Weir was a technician and so was Oatess. He worked with his players on individual offensive and defensive moves, the pick-and-roll, and the drop step to the basket. And then there were the basic man-to-man defense and a variety of zone defenses. His teams also learned the full-court press. Oatess's skill as a coach built both outstanding players and winning teams.

The prize, of course, for any coach, but especially for a local kid, was to be at the helm of the Marion Giants basketball team. Weir had taken two teams to the state finals. But he had not brought home the trophy as that long-ago, almost mystical 1926 team had done. Weir's two successors—Paul Weaver and John Givens—had not fared well either. Even though both men knew basketball and had teams with above average talent, neither coach could get to the state finals of Hoosier basketball—that four-tier, four-week process that culminated in the crowning of a state champion in Indianapolis. One coach made it to the Fort Wayne semi-state, and then faltered.

Weaver went on to become principal of Marion High School, while Givens moved to the college ranks and eventually coached the American Basketball Association's Kentucky Colonels basketball team. The head-coaching job in Marion became available in 1965, ten years after Oatess had worn the Giants' purple and gold school colors. He had established himself as an impressive winner with junior high and freshmen teams in the early 1960s. By rights, Oatess should have been a contender for the varsity coaching job. But he never got an interview. It went to a county coach who over the next several seasons—with talented teams taught and trained by Oatess—was unable to capture a state championship.

Although a successful junior high school and freshman coach, Oatess was not even selected to be the assistant/junior varsity coach. This team, comprised of sophomores, was known as the Little Giants. The new head coach did call Oatess to his office to inform him that someone else had been chosen for the assistant coaching job. He was told that he had "that uncanny ability to develop young athletes" and that his talents would be better suited at the ninth grade level. The junior varsity coaching job went to one of Oatess's former high school teammates. Two years younger than Oatess, the teammate had a modest win/loss record that did not compare to Archey's sixty-four wins against seven losses. No Marion team won the state title until the 1970s and 1980s, when Coach Bill Green won the state championship five times.

* * *

The year I was born, 1949, Mr. Archey was a seventh grader. While he was attending school on the north side of Marion, I was growing up nine blocks west of downtown Marion "on the hill." Our home was a two-story, green-shingled house with a small backyard and even smaller front yard. Horace Mann Elementary School and Martin Boots Junior High School were two blocks east of my home. I walked to school every day. I was never included in the basketball games with the other kids during my early elementary school years, although I did join the YMCA to play some basketball and swim. I first had the chance to play organized basketball when my family moved to a new housing addition on the northwest side of town. Before all the lots on the street were filled with new homes, there was a basketball goal planted in the tree lawn facing the street. It sat right in front of the Marion Giants basketball coach's home. Paul Weaver, successor to Woody Weir, could sit in his living room and keep an eye on the local talent. I doubt, though, that he paid much attention to the skinny fifth grader who just moved in across the street.

While seemingly a cliché, basketball truly has always been an integral part of Hoosier life. Each March in the 1950s and 1960s we would watch the state finals on television. There was Jimmy Rayl of Kokomo, the Van Arsdale twins (Tom and Dick) of Indianapolis Manual High School, and of course Oscar Robertson of Indianapolis Crispus Attucks and his coach, the legendary Ray Crowe. My buddies and I all wanted to be Marion

Giants. A friend and I attended the high school games as sixth graders in the Memorial Coliseum. Imitating the warm-up jackets and knee socks of the Giants, we purchased sweatshirts and high-top socks to wear at our elementary basketball games. We all tried to shoot our layups like the Giants and wanted to wear jersey number 40—the number worn by Harold Curdy, the star of the Giants.

Until the early 1960s, Marion High School was located on the Nelson Street hill, about four or five blocks north of Martin Boots and Horace Mann schools. We would often see the basketball players at the nearby YMCA or in downtown hamburger joints. It always surprised us to see them in street clothes, wearing watches, and talking to girls. This didn't seem like the behavior of guys who played the game of basketball. We didn't wear watches or talk to girls. And while we wore regular clothes, the only time we had seen the Giants was in uniform on the basketball court.

As I looked toward attending junior high school, I wondered if I would have a chance to make the team. I had grown, practiced more, and started on my Riverside Rockets Elementary "A" team as both a fifth and sixth grader. But now I would be competing against kids on a team that just three years earlier I had been unable to even try out for.

* * *

When the Marion basketball job did not come his way, Oatess began to explore possibilities outside Marion. Crowe requested that his superintendent offer Oatess the job of assistant basketball coach at his Indianapolis school. When the new Marion superintendent, Bernard McKenzie, heard of this, he contacted Oatess and basically promised him the next open head-coaching slot that met his credentials. Oatess finally received a head-coaching job in the Marion school system, but it was not to be in basketball. The call came from McKenzie to Oatess, but the offer was for the head job in track and cross-country, neither major sports. Nevertheless, he decided to take the assignments.

In both of these sports, Oatess used what he would call his "threshold of pain theory." At one point he looked into obtaining a patent for the unique approach. He had fashioned the idea from hearing about a runner in Europe who held onto trams to pace himself and also a man in the United States who used an automobile with a handle-type apparatus. Oatess transferred these basic thoughts into a practical theory of how people really ran.

Runners, as would be expected, slow down when pain hits them. Oatess believed that runners could "break through" that initial pain. If so they might gain what some have called a second wind, or at least a diminishing of the agony. On a traditional quarter-mile track, runners exerted more effort on the front stretch, where the coaches and crowd were, to urge them on. But on the backstretch the pain often got to the best of them, and they slowed down.

To counteract this phenomenon Oatess devised a new approach. Using a car with towropes, he would be with his runners to pull them through the pain barrier. Using math formulas and charts, he calculated the pace of a four-minute mile (fifteen miles per hour) and then reduced the figure to a reasonable time for his high school runners. Archey used twelve miles per hour as a benchmark so his runners would know what it would take to hit that mark. He would urge them on as coaches traditionally do, but also shout, "Don't let it pull you!" In four years he took a weak Marion track-and-field team to state prominence.

Oatess later published an article on his "towrope/threshold of pain" approach and was always on the lookout for other creative ideas. In basketball, Weir had "dribbling glasses." The lower part of empty eyeglass frames had protrusions that kept players from looking down when they were dribbling the ball up the court. Oatess improved on that concept by putting black tape on the bottom portion of the frames to achieve the same result. In cross-country, he used elevation in practice, directing his runners up the small hills in neighborhoods around the Marion Coliseum. And since most runners could not afford muscle building ankle weights, his runners wore old rubber boots.

As in basketball, the issue of race also emerged in track and field. On a road trip to Chrysler Field in New Castle, Indiana, the school bus pulled off at a roadside restaurant. The coaches thought it would be a good place to feed the team on its return to Marion after the meet. Oatess, the head coach, and one of his assistants jumped off the bus

Coach Oatess Archey poses with members of his 1968 track team that reached the state finals in such events as the long jump, hurdles, relays, and dashes.

and ran in to ask if the restaurant could handle forty athletes at about 6 p.m. The waitress, ignoring Oatess, looked at the assistant white coach and said, "Yes, we can handle that." The loyal assistant coach replied politely, but firmly, "Ma'am, HE [pointing to Oatess] is the head coach."

Taking programs in very bad shape, Oatess had built four winning teams in four years. He was nominated as Indiana Track Coach of the Year in 1969 and produced fifteen athletes who participated in the state track finals. With the head coaching job in basketball not open and his coaching successes in track and field at a pinnacle, Oatess entertained an offer to move to the college ranks. Almost twenty years later he told the local Marion newspaper, "Knowing I would never be head basketball coach at Marion, I decided it would be best for me to pack my bag and leave home." It was Ball State University that gave him his chance. "I couldn't do it in Marion," Oatess said. "Other people were giving me a chance when my own people weren't."

Two other former Marion High School coaches, Wave Myers and Al Faunce, had shifted from high school to college coaching. They were part of the football program at Ball State University in nearby Muncie, Indiana. Both Myers and Faunce were instrumental in assisting Oatess in landing the Ball State job. He weighed the offer in his mind and, with his wife's concurrence, decided to make the move. As assistant track and cross-country coach, Oatess specialized in the sprint, hurdles, and medley running events. In addition he served as an assistant professor of physical education.

Three weeks after arriving at Ball State University in the fall of 1969, the man who had hired Oatess left for another position. The university offered the newly arrived coach from Marion High School the head track and field job. Oatess declined, but suggested his friend Jerry Rushton from Earlham College in Richmond, Indiana, for the job. During their four years together in Muncie, these two men took the track program to the next level in terms of success and sophistication. Among the outstanding athletes they developed was steeplechaser Alan Myers, who received an invitation to the 1972 Olympic trials. Shortly after his "breaking the pain barrier" article was published, Oatess became assistant department head of Ball State's physical education department.

Archey checks the times of his cross-country runners during a meet in 1967.

What was the key to Oatess's success in basketball, track, and cross-country at both the high school and college level? The fundamental component of his philosophy was fairness. Due in large part to his own background and upbringing, this value shaped Oatess's coaching, teaching, and professional life. Being fair meant no partiality, no unearned privilege. Intruding parents in the gym were not welcome, no parental influence would be tolerated, and there were no breaks given for those with social distinction. Oatess played the best players, regardless of their race or their parents' status in the community. It is not an easy task to place fairness at the center of one's actions. But for Oatess it worked and worked well.

* * *

Just as Coach Archey never got to be the head coach of the Marion Giants basketball team, I never got to be a Marion Giant. I was cut from the team my senior year. I did run varsity cross-country for Mr. Archey and received a letter sweater. Never a strong runner, I did serve as the team's "rabbit." I would take off on the two-mile run in an attempt to have runners on the other team attempt to keep up with my pace. Unable to keep up with the pace myself, I would then fade to the back of the pack. Then our best runners would emerge, often passing the opposing team who had burned themselves out chasing me.

I have on occasion wondered what would have happened if Mr. Archey had gotten that head coaching job. Might I have had a chance to fulfill my boyhood dream and wear the purple and gold of the Marion High School basketball Giants? I like to think I would.

9

The FBI Years

Oatess Archey's professional career took a dramatic and unexpected turn in 1973. In that year he was recruited by the Federal Bureau of Investigation. A former Marion teacher had become an FBI agent and told Oatess that the Bureau was actively and genuinely recruiting blacks to become agents. After graduating from the FBI Academy in 1973, Oatess was assigned to the Detroit, Michigan, FBI Field Division. While in Michigan, he was trained by a former Olympic pistol shooting team member. Oatess had, in fact, never before shot a gun, even for sport or recreation. He discovered that using a firearm was truly an art.

In 1976 Oatess received a transfer to the FBI training center at Quantico, Virginia. While at Quantico, he served as a physical fitness and defensive tactics instructor. In 1986 he became the chief firearms instructor at FBI Headquarters in Washington, D.C. Oatess became so proficient with firearms that he was featured on the cover of *Jet* magazine on July 7, 1986. The caption read, "Black man becomes FBI firearms expert."

The FBI is the federal government's domestic police force. And the FBI that Oatess joined in 1973 was a much different institution than the one he retired from twenty years later. The year 1972 marked the end of an era when longtime FBI director, J. Edgar Hoover, died.

First known as the Bureau of Investigation, the agency was part of the Department of Justice and became home to the young Hoover in 1917. He worked his way up the system to the position of director in 1924 at the age of twenty-four. A squat, bulldog-like man, Hoover was a lawyer by training. And in the late 1920s and early 1930s he led the bureau to national fame by chasing and usually capturing gangsters, kidnappers, and bank robbers. These new legendary criminals included George "Baby Face" Nelson, Alvin Karpis, Charles "Pretty Boy" Floyd, John Dillinger, "Ma" Barker's Gang, and Bonnie Parker and Clyde Barrow.

These larger-than-life public figures, especially the Indiana-born Dillinger, captured the interest of the American people and the press with their criminal exploits. Then in 1932 famed aviator Charles Lindbergh's infant son was kidnapped and killed. The kidnapper, Bruno Richard Hauptmann, was captured and convicted of the crime in 1934. Hoover's bureau, using scientific crime detection methods to solve the case, gained the agency even greater renown and prominence. Although maintaining his innocence to the end, Hauptmann was executed.

At first the Bureau included agents who were mainly lawyers and accountants. Hoover would, in a brief eighteen months, transform the organization into a nationally renowned institution, newly named the Federal Bureau of Investigation. Deskbound agents began carrying guns and were eventually able to outthink and outmaneuver these well-known gangsters. "G Men," or government men, as the FBI agents became known, were heroes during the Great Depression. In movie houses, newspapers, on the radio, and even in comic books, they became almost mythic figures to the public.

In addition to winning fame for relentlessly pursuing major crooks,

Hoover and the FBI monitored potential internal foreign threats, especially Communists. This work took place during and after World War II. The search for what was labeled the "Red Menace" reached a peak with the "witch hunts" of the 1950s. Hoover's own career became synonymous with his unfaltering anti-Communist stance. The crime-busting defender of America public image did much to conceal the more controversial methods of the FBI that came to light after Hoover's death in May 1972.

Prize-winning historian David Kennedy has written that Hoover's obsession with communism led him into areas such as the Vietnam peace movement. With the blessing of President Lyndon B. Johnson, peace groups were sabotaged through "black bag break ins" by FBI agents of their headquarters and offices. Kennedy has written that these "clandestine tactics made the FBI look like a totalitarian state's secret police rather than a guardian of American democracy." This behavior by Hoover mirrored his work in 1919 and 1920 when he took part in the Justice Department raids of alleged "Reds" or Communists.

Recent historians of the civil rights movement, such as Taylor Branch and David J. Garrow, have documented that FBI practices included the use of wiretaps on telephones, questionable surveillance of American citizens by Bureau agents, and the collection of gossip on politicians and prominent figures in public life. This dubious information was even collected on American presidents, most notably John F. Kennedy. Hoover did not limit his investigations to occupants of the White House. After Hoover's death in 1972, *Time* magazine reported, "There was more than a tinge of racism in Hoover's vicious vendetta against Martin Luther King, Jr." The FBI director attempted to discredit the public work of the black civil rights leader by using agents to pry into his personal life. Hoover apparently truly believed that King's organization had connections to Communists. While still a controversial charge, *Time* magazine believed that Hoover crossed the legal and ethical line on numerous occasions in his investigation of the civil rights movement. According to *Time*, Hoover had to be pushed into hiring black agents.

Oatess became African American agent number eighty-five in 1973 out of a total force of 8,500 agents. Three years later, less than twenty black agents had been added. The former teacher and coach merely viewed all this as another hurdle to overcome. For years, Hoover had personally limited the number of black agents serving in the FBI. Until the early 1960s, there had been only five black FBI agents. And these men had not been agents in the true sense of the term. Raised in the segregated city of Washington, D.C., Hoover, according to biographer Richard Gid Powers, held the view of many southerners that whites should not provide any type of personal service for another white. This included cleaning, cooking, and chauffeuring. During World War II, Hoover had made his personal black employees FBI agents so they could be deferred from service in the armed forces.

Before the arrival of Kennedy in the White House in 1961, most men in the FBI viewed the agency as an all-white bastion. The idea that President Kennedy and his brother, Attorney General Robert Kennedy, would allow a black to become an authentic agent was never considered as even a remote possibility. Inside the FBI racial slurs were common. Powers noted that FBI agents, imitating the New England accent of the Kennedy brothers, would say, "Boys if you don't work with 'vigah,' you'll be replaced by a n _ _ _ _ h." One agent estimated that in 1960, 90 percent of the time bureau personnel used the repugnant, highly offensive, and well-known racial slur rather than the acceptable term at that time, Negro.

Powers and other historians have reported that with the arrival of the Kennedys things changed. As head of the Justice Department and therefore Hoover's immediate superior, Robert Kennedy began to pressure Hoover by asking how many black agents there were in the bureau. The director told others that he had held his ground with Kennedy on this issue. Hoover repeatedly told the attorney general that by hiring blacks he would be lowering bureau qualifications. That meant that any standard that blacks could meet would be too low for him. To his face, Hoover never did tell Robert Kennedy about the five "agents" who were all employed in personal service to him. Due to this pressure, however, Hoover grudgingly hired five black agents by the end of 1962.

Current high school and college history textbooks describe the stance of Hoover and the FBI at this time. Part of Hoover's problem with blacks had to do with his personal view that the civil rights movement of the 1950s and 1960s was a front for Communist activity. Hoover appeared to have a long-standing dislike of black organizations in general. As a young man, he had been a central figure in the campaign between 1919 and 1923 that shattered the Black Nationalist Movement. Its leader Marcus Garvey was jailed and eventually deported to Africa. Hoover had weighed in again during the 1950s. Under the guise of "fact finding," he provided reports to President Dwight Eisenhower's cabinet that supported many southern concerns over the advances being made in desegregation.

J. Edgar Hoover.

The FBI investigated, and on occasion, broke some of the racially motivated crimes during the civil rights movement. But, according to historians Branch and Garrow, the bureau did little to protect the workers in the movement or prevent the violence that occurred in the 1960s. Instead Hoover directed his attention to King, attempting to break the civil rights leader through threats and intimidation. Only King's assassination in 1968 brought an end to Hoover's personal vendetta against the Nobel Prize–winning civil rights leader.

In his book *Broken: The Troubled Past and Uncertain Future of the FBI*, Powers argued that Hoover left the agency weaker due to his excesses. In the end this was bad for the country. Powers suggests that the criticism of the agency went too far, crippling the FBI for a decade after Hoover's death. This made it impossible for the Bureau to function effectively with emerging challenges such as terrorism.

Criticizing the FBI in any way has often been seen as being disloyal to America and the institution itself. During the Watergate scandals and downfall of President Richard Nixon, *Washington Post* journalist Bob Woodward had a secret informant inside the government. This person provided the reporter with clues to the unraveling of the Watergate scandals. For thirty years, Woodward kept the identity of his source a secret. Then in 2005, onetime number two man at the FBI, Mark Felt, went public claiming that he was the clandestine informer code-named "Deep Throat." Woodward confirmed this. Felt's reluctance to come forward was due to his concern that his actions would be viewed as disloyalty to the Bureau. Others, though, saw his actions as serving to expose corruption in the highest reaches of the American government. Agents today still feel that tug of loyalty, even to Hoover.

One such man who maintains that the FBI's activities were legitimate and necessary is Cartha "Deke" DeLoach. The former agent and head of public relations at the bureau, in a 2004 interview, said that the "FBI has gotten a very bad rap over the years." As Hoover would often say, the agency was an information gathering organization, not a policy-making entity. DeLoach claimed that the FBI was active in civil rights cases and did face down the Ku Klux Klan at times. Others, referring to the taping of King's telephone conversations and attempting to pass them off to the press to embarrass the civil rights leader, remain critical. Former *Washington Post* editor Ben Bradlee has accused DeLoach of approaching him to publish the tapes, a charge that the former agent denied.

In the post-Hoover era, when Oatess became an agent, the FBI had become a more hospitable workplace. After his first assignments in Michigan, Virginia, and the District of Columbia, he rose to the rank of Supervisory Special Agent in the FBI Criminal Investigative Division. From there he became the Unit Chief over the FBI Police Force and in-house security force at the Hoover Building in Washington, D.C. His career with the FBI mirrored the major cases that the bureau handled during Agent Archey's twenty-year tenure. It was Archey who took the phone call from the U.S. Secret Service at FBI headquarters that President Ronald Reagan had been shot by a would-be assassin in early 1981. It was not the first or the last high-profile case he would be involved in during his FBI years.

One of the best-known cases in the mid 1970s was the kidnapping of Patty Hearst, the granddaughter of the wealthy publisher William Randolph Hearst. The elder Hearst owned a number of newspapers from New York to Chicago to San Francisco. In 1973 a gang of California radicals calling themselves the Symbionese Liberation Army kidnapped Patty, a college student at the time. Their leader was known as Cinque. Stationed in Detroit, Oatess and a fellow agent followed leads in the case that included interviewing Patty's college roommate in Ann Arbor, Michigan.

Oatess Archey poses with FBI Director Clarence M. Kelley, circa 1974.

Another assignment Archey was given during his FBI career was the pursuit of D. B. Cooper, the thief who parachuted out of a jetliner with an enormous amount of cash strapped to his back and was never found. Eventually Archey was assigned to Los Angeles, known as the "bank robbery capital of the world." Archey was, just before his retirement, on the trail of Theodore Kaczynski, the elusive man who mailed bombs to government employees. The press would label Kaczynski the "Unabomber."

Even in the post-Hoover days in the agency, the issue of race emerged. When on cases with a white partner, Oatess would often be ignored by white suspects being interviewed on investigations. They would look right past him and speak directly to the white agent. A female colleague one day complained about her freckles. "How would you like to be one big brown freckle?" replied Oatess. His race, even in his position of responsibility and respect, made him a target for ridicule or derision. After an investigation, it was not unusual for the FBI field office to receive a call lodging a complaint that a black man—Oatess—had been at their door or in the neighborhood impersonating an agent. "Why would you think he was doing that?" the FBI agent receiving the call would ask. "Because he wasn't white," was the usual answer.

Over the years of Archey's service, though, the FBI made progress. The number of female agents and agents of color increased, and as society advanced on the issue of race so did the agency.

As Archey pondered retirement, he considered the possibility of using the skills he had learned in the FBI to serve as a security consultant in Southern California, where his sons lived. In fact, he eventually kept watch over such figures as singer Whitney Houston, saxophonist Kenny G, and soccer player Pele. After retiring from the bureau in 1993, Archey said—referring to a Whitney Houston and Kevin Costner movie titled *The Bodyguard*—that in fact he was the *real* bodyguard, absent the film's romantic element. On the final day of the men's World Cup Soccer in 1994 at the Rose Bowl in Pasadena, California, Oatess escorted several celebrities to the center of the playing field. He did so with more than 100,000 fans in attendance as they watched the halftime entertainment. Reflecting on his custodial job in Marion, Indiana, after college, Oatess thought to himself, "from the 'toilet bowl' to the Rose Bowl."

* * *

I had seen Mr. Archey one time at Ball State University just before he left to join the FBI (I did not know he was going to the Bureau). He was still coaching and teaching at the university, and I had a brief visit with him in his office. He shared with me some stories of his teaching and coaching in Muncie with college students and had a few words of advice about teaching for me. I was now in my first year as a teacher in our hometown of Marion. I started my career in education at McCullough Junior High School, where Mr. Archey had also begun teaching a decade before. Ironically, while it was whites that initially kept him out of teaching, it was a black man that supported my obtaining a teaching position. An African American podiatrist, Doctor Joseph Casey, school board member and customer at my father's service station, had put in a good word for me with a principal and the personnel director of the school system. I received an interview and the position.

For the next twenty-five years there would be no contact between Mr. Archey and me. I may have written to him once in California in the early 1990s, but I don't remember how I got his address or what I said. I do know that he answered me.

10

The Courthouse Square — Revisited

The word retirement is one that may eventually fall out of fashion. As the longevity of the American population increases and citizens remain active in their careers, the term could eventually lose its relevance. Maybe the designation should be known as transition.

Retirement certainly did not come easily for Oatess Archey at the close of his career in the Federal Bureau of Investigation. He was called on to serve in high-level security positions with Hollywood stars and celebrities, the 1994 World Cup Soccer games, and also at the 1996 Atlanta Olympics. Jobs in the security arena and in California were plentiful and often exotic. Life after leaving the FBI was comfortable for the former agent. Residing in sunny Southern California near his two sons, life was good. Both sons had burgeoning careers, one in acting and the other in computer technology management for the Veterans' Administration. But after a life of nonstop activity, retirement seemed premature for an energetic man who was still in his fifties.

The idea of returning to Marion, Indiana, and Grant County may have begun as a family matter. Due to health problems, Barbara Archey's mother was in need of increasing assistance. But then another idea emerged. It was evident that Oatess—the self-described "little engine that could"—sought another challenge, not merely retirement checks. Oatess still believed he could make a difference, and from that motivation his wife, Barbara, fashioned the idea of "giving back." But give back to whom, and perhaps more importantly, where?

Then a series of events occurred that made the answer to the question "where" clearer. In 1997 Oatess returned to Marion to speak at a law enforcement dinner followed by a National Association for the Advancement of Colored People luncheon talk. Other honors quickly followed: a scholarship in his name, a teachers' organization award, the key to the city of Marion, and finally a Sagamore of the Wabash designation from the Indiana governor's office. "Maybe it's time to go home," Oatess told a writer. "Maybe people want me to come home and get involved."

Oatess Archey speaks to a crowd during his tenure as Grant County sheriff.

Law enforcement at this time was a changing profession. And despite at times a troubled history, the FBI remained the premier law enforcement agency in the world. Could the knowledge, skills, and experiences that Oatess had gained on the national level be translated to service in his hometown and surrounding communities? Matching these areas of expertise with his commitment, he decided to find out. Oatess and Barbara decided that they would try to give back to their home community—Marion—the place over the years that had treated them in such a mixed fashion.

Oatess's former high school teammate, Norm Jones, has suggested that Oatess returned to try to correct injustices from the past. "Oatess was different. He seemed very serious and gave the impression he was always on the watch for fear of doing something that might provoke racial tension," Jones said. "He was observant to the point that he tried to understand what was behind the discrimination and what, if anything, could be done to make things better in Marion."

While city police chiefs are political appointments in Indiana municipalities, the office of county sheriff is an elected one. The position of Grant County sheriff was going to be open in January 1999, and the countywide office would be decided through the process of a spring primary and a November general election in 1998. Although a political independent, Oatess decided to explore what his chances might be in the political arena. Grant County was a Republican county that had elected, on occasion, a few Democrats to office. Oatess contacted Tom Wise, his high school friend and confidant. Wise had connections to the Democratic Party, and there was an interest on the part of key party members to a possible candidacy by Oatess. It would be an uphill battle, but the Archeys were going back home.

When Oatess retired from the FBI, his son Marlon said that the family exhaled a collective sigh of relief. Through many high-profile cases, difficult, and often dangerous situations, the father and husband had completed his career in the Bureau unscathed. It was understandable then, that the thought of him going back into law enforcement did not thrill the family. For Oatess, though, "there was apprehension about coming home," more than concern about physical danger.

Barriers were mentioned that might hamper a run for political office. Oatess had left Marion in early 1969. Political races are traditionally won through name recognition. Connections to the community and financial commitments from citizens in support of the candidate are also needed. Oatess had been away for over a quarter of a century and these elements for political success might not be present. Two potential roadblocks were raised. First, there was his lack of political experience, as he had never before run for public office. Second, there was the question whether a bona fide connection existed between his experiences in the FBI and the job of local law enforcement. The latter included everything from patrolling county roads to the administration and supervision of a jail. Oddly, at the same time, there was even the question as to whether the former FBI agent might be overqualified to be a county sheriff.

Then, as might have been expected, there was the issue of race. No black had ever been elected sheriff in Indiana, let alone Grant County with its troubled history in race relations. Wise believed that racism was still very much in evidence. Although Wise thought that his friend had a chance of winning the city vote, he thought Oatess would have a much more difficult time carrying a county that was overwhelmingly white. In addition, county sheriff offices were viewed as less progressive in race relations than their city police counterparts.

Oatess at first was also skeptical and did not see how a successful campaign could be run with so little political expertise and limited

Archey on the stump during his 2002 re-election campaign for sheriff.

time. Barbara again bolstered his confidence. She believed that he could succeed. But it was also Oatess's own inner strength. "I've been jumping hurdles my whole life," he told an interviewer. "I consider myself the Little Engine that could." The situation was similar to what they had faced during their first return to Marion almost forty years earlier. And so Barbara and Oatess moved ahead to meet the challenges they knew they would face in their hometown.

Cynthia Carr, a New York writer with Marion roots, had returned to write about the 1930 lynching. In her view, Oatess "projected a quiet authority. Gray-haired with gold rimmed glasses, he was an ex-athlete who still looked fit and seemed younger than his sixty years." She observed him giving campaign volunteers and the youth of the city pep talks. Oatess spoke of possibilities and of everyone winning if he won. Carr believed that the racial harmony that so many spoke of across the nation was truly evident in Oatess's campaign headquarters. This was seen in the fact that Oatess even had two campaign managers, one white and one black.

Oatess was advised by many friends to build a coalition, and not to campaign by what is called mudslinging or negative comments toward the opponent. His campaign theme was "People First." He spoke often of his qualifications and he looked like a winner. Running against a former student in the Democratic primary in the spring of 1998, he won 65 percent of the vote to his opponent's 35 percent. After this victory in the spring, Oatess prepared for the fall campaign.

That fall in the election he faced another one of his former students, Mike Back, who was a twenty-five year veteran of the Sheriff's Department and held the rank of captain. Although both men were experienced law-enforcement professionals, Oatess had been absent from the county for twenty-nine years. This is where the idea of a coalition proved critical to his success. The race ultimately depended on the level of support Oatess received from the students, athletes, friends, and former colleagues whose lives he had touched as a coach and teacher in Marion.

One man, Larry Myers, was representative of those who came forward to support and contribute to the Archey for Sheriff campaign. Coach Archey, at Marion High School in the 1960s, had three strong legs on his shuttle hurdling relay team. But he needed a fourth. He reached down and plucked out a young man, Myers, someone who could not seem to master the all-important timing of his steps between the hurdles. Archey put his confidence in Myers and the uncertain hurdler stepped up as the fourth member of the relay team. His efforts gave the Giants' track team a victory at an indoor meet held at Indiana University.

That confidence was something that Myers, now a successful businessman in the city, never forgot. He told this story at a "Welcome Home Oatess Archey" dinner. Myers added that a black coach had looked beyond color, something that both blacks and whites can often find difficult to do. And the coach won with a predominantly white track team, just as he had done with junior high basketball teams.

Oatess told Myers that it was going to be a difficult and close election and pondered aloud what his chances might be. Myers responded that Oatess had put his faith in a struggling hurdler and how deeply Myers had not wanted to let his coach down. Myers said that as a bank executive he had used the Oatess Archey philosophy. He had put faith in his employees and never regretted emulating his mentor. Now as an adult, Myers did not want to let his former coach down. "Hey, Coach," said Myers, "you are going to win. A bunch of gray-haired, varicose veined women and balding, potbellied men who were your students, athletes, and friends are going to put you over the top. We saw you as a coach, not a black man." Oatess took this idea into his race for sheriff. "Your friends are a reflection of you," he later said. He spoke of friends, not just black friends.

While at the FBI Oatess told tour guides to be careful with the words they used when giving tours of the agency's headquarters building. Phrases or words like "you people" and "them" or "those guys" can hurt. In fact, one of his favorite sayings is "Hate hurts." Another saying he often used was "People don't care how much you know until they know how much you care." The former agent firmly believed that a person's character was not based on race. There were good people, and unfortunately some not-so-good people, in every ethnic group.

The campaign was competitive and run professionally in both camps. Yet a side comment had even been made that if elected Oatess would appoint all blacks to positions or be highly politically partisan. But the Democratic Party did work hard for its candidate. Former Democratic mayors Tony Maidenburg and Robert Mitchell, both successful and popular officeholders, gave Oatess their endorsements, as did other state office holders from Grant County. As Myers had predicted, the coalition of his former students and friends turned out on election day.

The election, held on November 2, 1998, proved to be exceptionally close. When the polls closed, Oatess held an 8 percent lead, but that slim advantage eroded all evening until there was less than 2 percent separating the candidates. "Hey, I'm a competitor," Oatess said as the votes slowly came in from around the county. Referring to a political contest, not an athletic one, he went on to say, "When I get in a race, I want to win very badly. That's what my life has been all about. To be a winner." When almost all the precincts had reported, Oatess remained in the lead by six hundred votes, with two hundred absentee markers still out. By ten o'clock that night, though, his victory was assured. The final tally was 10,778 to 10,198.

The headlines that Oatess had been denied when he was a state champion track star were finally his. "Historic Victory for Archey" blared across the top of the front page of the Wednesday morning, November 3, 1998, edition of the *Marion Chronicle-Tribune.* "Archey has night of firsts, becomes state's first black sheriff" read the subheadline. The story began, "In nail-biting fashion, a former FBI agent and Marion native won the Grant County sheriff's race Tuesday to become the first black sheriff in Indiana history." Although the vote was close, no recount was sought. "They said it couldn't happen," said Oatess. "Some say when you leave home, you can't come back. That's not true." Grant County had indeed elected Indiana's first black sheriff in its 183-year history.

The victory deeply and emotionally moved the usually stoic Oatess. Choking back tears, he turned from the crowd of his supporters and handed the microphone to his wife. Barbara quickly quipped, "I guess I have to take over." Barbara's support has been a recurring theme in Oatess's life. "She is my best friend and has been there all the way," he later said of his wife as tears streamed down his face. Speaking of all the challenges he had faced in his life, Barbara said of her husband, "I just wanted him to keep going. I knew there were better things for him."

Senior writer, Mike Cline, analyzing the race in the *Marion Chronicle-Tribune*, concluded that voters had a choice between two highly qualified candidates and had obviously given the race much thought. "A Democrat does not win a countywide race in Grant County without some Republican support," Cline wrote. Of all the races on that election day, the sheriff's contest drew the most interest and participation. Dissecting the election results, Oatess put race aside as an issue and noted, "When a lot of people said you can't, I said I could. They said it was impossible—you can't win. The county is 91 percent white, you are black. Well, I didn't believe it." He added when interviewed, "Black and white people voted for the man, not the black man."

When does a person ultimately arrive at a final destination? If it is a trip from one place to another then the definition of "arriving" is fairly simple. If it means merely showing up, then again it is easy to discern if a person is present or not present. But what does it mean for a person to finally arrive in a lifelong journey? To feel a sense of completeness, fulfillment, and of being in the right place at the right time? Oatess Archey had to feel that he had finally arrived when he was elected sheriff. He reflected on his father's words, "It doesn't matter where you come from in life, but it's where you are going in life that counts."

It seemed that the newly elected sheriff was going to become an instant celebrity. In addition to statewide coverage of his election, there were calls from television talk-show host Montel Williams, *Applause* magazine, and even inquiries as to possible book offers to tell his life story. Oatess remembered a woman saying after the lynching, "One day there will be a time when a sheriff won't be a white man." She was right. There was additional irony in the fact that one of Oatess's predecessors in the office, Tony George, had shot his great-grandfather while he was a Marion policeman.

Oatess was sworn into office in the Marion High School Auditorium on January 1, 1999. The event captured statewide attention. This was, in part, due to the fact that James Cameron, the youth who had escaped the lynch mob sixty-eight years earlier, attended the ceremony. He had driven to Marion from his home in Wisconsin. (Cameron founded America's Black Holocaust Museum in Milwaukee, Wisconsin, to educate the public about racism and episodes such as the Marion lynching.) There would also be atonement when Cameron received an official pardon from the governor of the state.

An Indiana historian, James Madison, in his book *A Lynching in the Heartland*, linked Cameron with newly elected Sheriff Archey. The connection was by line of succession from the ineffective Depression-era sheriff, Jake Campbell, to the new sheriff, Oatess Archey. Madison described the new sheriff as "handsome, tall, still athletic-looking, immaculately dressed . . . polished and articulate" in a new brown sheriff's uniform. The historian noted that the "long line of history" was not lost on the numerous members of the press.

Madison interviewed Archey early in his term. The new occupant of the office looked out of his window at the old, abandoned Grant County Jail and remarked that it was a reminder for him to count his blessings. It also demonstrated how much the county had changed. The new sheriff also made it clear that due to his qualifications no one could label him a "token" or use race as the reason he had won. He did observe to Madison that he would not pretend that the past was dead. Some citizens had told him that their votes for him "helped clear consciences" and "do the right thing this time." He told another interviewer that the courthouse square as well as the jail had been symbolic. The tree on the site that was used for lynchings had stood for many years as a silent reminder to young black males—"If you 'crossed the line,' this is what could happen to you."

Oatess later traveled to Wisconsin when the University of Wisconsin at Milwaukee honored Cameron with an honorary degree. Archey called Cameron a pioneer and said, "I stand on his shoulders," noting that their lives had crossed in strange ways. After being sworn into office, Oatess, contrary to the campaign rhetoric of his opponents, was even-handed and fair in his appointments. For example, he appointed James Lugar, a Republican, who had returned from the Tucson, Arizona, police department, to serve as his deputy chief.

Although the election had been highly competitive and vigorously fought, the people had spoken and Oatess had been their choice. Being affirmed by one's friends and former students, most of all in one's hometown, is unquestionably gratifying. "My friend Oatess had come full circle as he moved from being dreadfully discriminated against as a youngster to a position whereby he would not allow such evil to take place in the town in which he grew up," noted Norm Jones.

In a sense, one never really arrives at a destination because no journey is complete. No one questioned Oatess's actual electoral victory, but there were agitators who had a notion that by attempting to provoke and produce skepticism and ridicule they could undermine the people's voice. The right of free speech is almost absolute in the United States and rightfully so. Narrow-minded citizens from outside the community were bused into Marion to see if the new sheriff's reputation could be damaged or at least tarnished.

Unfortunately, Indiana has never been found wanting for members in that "all-American" organization the Ku Klux Klan. The National Grand Dragon of the Klan once resided in Indiana, and activity at some level within the state seems to have been uninterrupted during most of the twentieth century. Early in Sheriff Archey's term, a group of Indiana Klanners came to Marion. They held a demonstration against the newly elected black sheriff. On the video that recorded the event, Klan rally chants can be heard such as, "Hate n _ _ _ _ _ s, hate Jews, white power."

In 2000 the actor Danny Glover featured Oatess in his television series *Courage* on the Fox Network. Each week Glover showcased men and women across the country who demonstrated heroic courage in their daily lives. The segment on Oatess documented his life and professional career ending with the Klan rally in Marion. Glover called

Top: *Archey lectures on law enforcement during his days as sheriff.* Left: *With his wife, Barbara, at his side Archey receives an honorary doctor of laws degree from Indiana Wesleyan University in 2001.*

the gathering a "hate rally." The program gave national attention to both Marion and its sheriff.

One march leader, using a loudspeaker, asked the small crowd of onlookers what they thought of their "Nee-gro" sheriff. A counterdemonstration actually took place with citizens holding signs declaring everything from support for their sheriff to tolerance for the marchers. James Cameron returned to Marion to support Oatess—an old man in the crowd sustaining his younger black brother. As for the sheriff himself, he and his fellow law enforcement women and men went about their jobs, assuring the safety of all supporters and protestors.

Some of the taunts did sting, though. Oatess later said that he could not entirely tune out their diatribes, which included hateful racial remarks that "white men should be extra careful to watch out for the well-being of their women" with a black man in a position of authority. Again one of the most long-standing stereotypes of black males was given voice. The long married, religious, and morally upright Oatess had to be thinking, "How can such things be said about me when they don't even know me?"

His son, Eugene Archey, later said that his father never spoke of disliking those who were dressed that day in the white Klan robes. Oatess had said when he took the sheriff's oath it was to protect all the people—even those who were demonstrating their hate for him. The sheriff's office employees were embarrassed by the crowd's racial slurs and tried to shield Archey from the Klan protesters. But in fact, Oatess actually felt sorry for them. Sorry that such hate could emerge toward a man they did not know at all.

* * *

After tracking Oatess Archey's win as sheriff through a friend in Marion over the Internet, I decided to visit my former coach and teacher.

I was in Indianapolis to see an automobile race and visit friends at Ball State University in Muncie. Going to Marion is something I always tried to do—placing flowers on my grandparents' grave, driving by the homes where I used to live, and taking a look at the schools where I attended and taught.

Without making an appointment or even calling, I parked on Adams Street and walked into the Willis Van Devanter Grant County Complex that housed the county jail and the sheriff's office. I walked up to the barred windows of the administrative offices and asked if Sheriff Archey was in. "Your name?" requested the secretary. I told her and she phoned the sheriff's office. Mispronouncing my name, she told Sheriff Archey I would like to see him. There was the incorrect repeating of my name several times and some muffled conversation on her part. Hanging up, she said, "He doesn't seem to know you."

Wondering if he really might not remember me—he did after all have a large number of students and had coached a number of sports—I decided to give it one more try. Carefully pronouncing my name again to the secretary, I asked if she would tell him that I was "one of his basketball boys." Patiently she phoned the sheriff's office one more time and almost immediately Mr. Archey bounded out of his office, had the security button on the locked door released, and welcomed me into his office. I came by to say hello and we talked for three hours. The years melted away and we were again walking the halls of Martin Boots Junior High School and Marion High School.

* * *

At times it no doubt seemed to the Marion community that the legacy of its racial history would never abate. In late 2004 professional basketball star Zach Randolph returned for a visit to his hometown. An all-state basketball player, Randolph had been a Marion Giant, spent one year at Michigan State University, and then signed with the National Basketball Association's Portland Trailblazers. Randolph, who had had some minor brushes with the law during his young adulthood in Marion, gave an interview with *ESPN: The Magazine*. One statement read, "Zach Randolph pretty much hates his hometown."

But there was also another side to the Randolph story. A guest columnist in the local paper responded strongly to the idea that his hometown was not hospitable and repudiated Randolph's assertions of ill treatment, indicating that the community had supported Randolph in many ways. There was an element of truth in this response. Numerous fans of Randolph drove to Indianapolis when Portland played the Indiana Pacers. It all seemed to show that the community of Marion was trying to rid itself of its negative image. It was also apparent that most of the community did not wish to revisit the atrocity of 1930.

In 2002 Oatess won reelection, but this time the vote was not even close. He took 74 percent of the popular vote in the general election. The vote of confidence was no surprise. Oatess had implemented a number of community-based policing programs and had been appointed to numerous statewide and national committees. He continued to run the department on the basis of his lifelong philosophy of fairness, caring, and holding people accountable.

Law enforcement is difficult and complex. So much of the work that is a part of the criminal justice system is closely intertwined with the community, especially the success of a leader and his or her team. Grant County, and especially the city of Marion, was in the midst of an economic tailspin. The jobless rate had doubled from 2000 to 2004. The decade from 1994 to 2004 had produced a decrease of manufacturing jobs from ten thousand to six thousand. The Thompson television factory, formerly the RCA plant, shut its doors in April 2004.

Often difficult economic times have an effect on other segments of society. The possibility of higher crime rates, family problems, and overall stress for individuals can all occur. Archey reported in June 2004 that the county jail population was at 310, which was fifty more than capacity. But he also noted that the number was not much higher than what usually occurred at that time of year. The veteran law enforcement professional was able to hold things steady in tough times.

The *Indianapolis Star* ran a two-part editorial cartoon on Marion's economic plight. Gary Varvel's cartoon, in color with multiple panels, gave an even-handed account of the pessimism and the optimism that the city of Marion was feeling at the time. Varvel called his cartoons "Welcome to Marion: A City Torn Between Hope and Despair." The future was left open with a youngster looking at a glass of water and wondering if it were half full or half empty. Varvel seemed to anticipate better days ahead.

The fact that Oatess returned to Marion seemed to endorse this idea. Although Marion continued to struggle with its past, Oatess concentrated on the community's assets and future. The Marion that had elected him sheriff could not have done so if it were still a racist place. His belief in the community, his deep roots in its educational institutions, and his expertise as educator, teacher, and leader all made the glass look half full. All leadership is about relationships. Oatess had built relationships from his days as a student, athlete, coach, teacher, law professional, and elected official.

Note of Oatess's accomplishments now began to be chronicled and fêted. *Indiana Blacks in the Twentieth Century*, published in 2000, relates the election of a highly qualified African American candidate for sheriff—Oatess—being elected by mostly white voters against the backdrop of Marion's grim history, and a distinguished photograph of Oatess closes the book. In 2002 Indiana Wesleyan University gave Oatess an honorary doctor of laws degree. The next year he appeared in an Indiana social studies textbook titled *Horizons* by Harcourt

Publishers. Oatess is named and pictured receiving a Governor's Award for Excellence in Public Safety. The narrative of the textbook tells about diversity and culture. In 2006 Oatess was one of the first seven Marion High School alumni to be honored in the school's Hall of Distinction.

When asked about the foundations of his success, the modest Oatess provides a number of answers. His parents and his faith are always at the top of his list. Oatess recalled once hearing a minister say that the most powerful position on earth is when you are on your knees praying to God. Oatess is a man of prayer himself and noted, "Through it all God has taken care of me."

What about the future? What about the youth of Marion? It's all about family values according to Oatess. "Vice President Dan Quayle may not have been able to spell potato," he said, "but he may have been right about the importance of family values." This includes conversation with kids at the supper table, board games, and family get-togethers. He also indicated that parents need to stay involved. "Know what's going on in the kids' rooms, with their friends, and on the Internet. Don't be afraid to discipline," he advised. "Listen to your children. If you don't, the bad guys will."

Oatess once stated to the city of Marion, "Thank you for trusting your kids with me," he said. He was honored that parents' most cherished possession, their children, were placed under his direction as both teacher and coach. Even in his role as sheriff, youth programs were central. The trust given was always understood by the coach, the teacher, the agent, and the elected official. He considers his election and re-election as sheriff as his most important accomplishment. He was the "people's choice." What he did with that trust for the youth of Marion, along with fairness and commitment, may be his greatest legacy.

* * *

I, too, returned to Marion briefly in the early 1980s to teach at the local college before moving on to administrative positions in the private sector and higher education. Reconnecting after his election, I invited my former teacher and coach to my university in Arkansas. I had asked him to open the school year by speaking to the faculty in the College of Education of which I was dean. He also took time to share his story and thoughts with a group of student teachers who were meeting before beginning their semester in the schools of the Mississippi Delta.

To my faculty, he spoke of tolerance: the need to impact lives with their own work and the need to always strive for justice and fairness in a world where those commodities were in short supply. When asked by a faculty member what he thought of his former student, who was now dean of the college, he glanced at me and humorously responded that he never thought he would see me leading such a gathering of notable professors.

What had I learned from this man? More than I had given ample time to consider. He had shown me that while race was an issue in American life, and probably would be far into the future, it need not paralyze a person's actions or force them to behave in a negative way. Mr. Archey, still Mr. Archey to me, never amputated the memory and memories of race from his own mind and his own life. But he never allowed it to be a barrier—a hurdle—either. Other values emerged as more important. These were fairness, civility, service to others, and never forgetting where one had come from.

To Mr. Archey, as we are taught, in the sight of God, all men and women however obscure are created with grace, dignity, and a touch of divinity. The boy whose father owned a two-pumper gas station next to the railroad tracks was as important to Mr. Archey as the son or daughter of the city's wealthy merchants, physicians, and attorneys. Mr. Archey's achievements, from the athletic fields to the classroom and finally to his law and political successes, while changing the world for those around him never changed his conviction in equality for all. And as a person, it never changed him in the slightest.

Learn More About Archey

Books

Paul S. Boyer. *The Enduring Vision: A History of the American People from 1865* (New York: Houghton Mifflin Company, 2004).

Taylor Branch. *At Canaan's Edge: America in the King Years, 1965–68* (New York: Simon and Schuster, 2006).

————. *Parting the Waters: America in the King Years, 1954–63* (New York: Simon and Schuster, 1988).

————. *Pillar of Fire: America in the King Years, 1963–65* (New York: Simon and Schuster, 1998).

James Cameron. *A Time of Terror* (Milwaukee, WS: TD Publications, 1982).

Cynthia Carr. *Our Town: A Heartland Lynching, a Haunted Town, and the Hidden History of White America* (New York: Crown Publishers, 2006).

Mildred B. G. Gallot. *A History of Grambling State University* (Lanham, MD: University Press of America, 1985).

David J. Garrow. *Bearing the Cross: Marin Luther King Jr. and the Southern Christian Leadership Conference* (New York: William Morrow and Company, 1986).

William Gildea. *Where the Game Matters Most: A Last Championship Season in Indiana High School Basketball* (Boston: Little Brown and Company, 1997).

Greg Guffey. *The Golden Age of Indiana High School Basketball* (Bloomington: Indiana University Press, 2006).

Phillip M. Hoose. *Hoosiers: The Fabulous Basketball Life of Indiana* (New York: Vintage Books, 1986).

Norman Jones. *Growing Up in Indiana: The Culture and Hoosier*

Hysteria Revisited (Bloomington, IN: Authorhouse Press, 2005).

David Kennedy and Lizabeth Cohen. *The American Pageant: A History of the Republic* (New York: Houghton Mifflin Company, 2002).

Rachel A. Koestler-Grack. *Going to School during the Civil Rights Movement* (Mankato, MN: Blue Earth Books, 2001).

Richard Kluger. *Simple Justice: The History of the* Brown v. Board of Education *and Black America's Struggle for Equality* (New York: Alfred A. Knopf, 2004).

Robert S. Lynd and Helen Merrell Lynd. *Middletown: A Study in Contemporary American Culture* (New York: Harcourt, Brace, and Company, 1929).

James H. Madison. *A Lynching in the Heartland: Race and Memory in America* (New York: Palgrave, 2001).

William Manchester. *The Glory and the Dream: A Narrative History of America, 1932–1972* (Boston: Little, Brown, and Company, 1973).

June R. McKown. *Marion: A Pictorial History* (St. Louis: G. Bradley Publishing, 1989).

Diane McWhorter. *A Dream of Freedom: The Civil Rights Movement from 1954 to 1968* (New York: Scholastic, 2004).

Richard Gid Powers. *Broken: The Troubled Past and Uncertain Future of the FBI* (New York: Free Press, 2004.)

————. *Secrecy and Power: The Life of J. Edgar Hoover* (New York: Free Press of Glencoe, 1987).

Randy Roberts. *"But They Can't Beat Us": Oscar Robertson and the Crispus Attucks Tigers* (Indianapolis: Indiana Historical Society, 1999).

Oscar Robertson. *The Big O: My Life, My Times, My Game* (New York: Rodale, 2003).

Herb Schwomeyer. *Hoosier Hysteria: A History of Indiana High School Basketball*, Fifth Edition (Greenfield, IN: Mitchell-Fleming Printing, 1982).

Harold M. Sherman. *Mayfield's Fighting Five* (New York: D. Appleton and Company, 1926).

————. *Get 'Em Mayfield* (New York: Grosset and Dunlap, 1927).

Emma Lou Thornbrough and Lana Ruegamer. *Indiana Blacks in the Twentieth Century* (Bloomington: Indiana University Press, 2000).

Bob Woodward. *The Secret Man: The Story of Watergate's Deep Throat* (New York: Simon and Schuster, 2005).

Richard Wormser. *The Rise and Fall of Jim Crow: The African-American Struggle Against Discrimination, 1865–1964* (New York: Franklin Watts Division of Grolier Publishing, 1999).

Newspapers

Indianapolis News.

Indianapolis Star.

Marion Chronicle.

Marion Chronicle-Tribune.

Marion Tribune.

Index